AFRICAN SLAVERY

Also by Edwin P. Hoyt

THE LAST EXPLORER:
The Adventures of Admiral Byrd

FRANKLIN PIERCE:
The Fourteenth President of the United States

JOHN TYLER

AFRICAN SLAVERY

Edwin P. Hoyt

ILLUSTRATED WITH PHOTOGRAPHS

Abelard-Schuman
New York London
An Intext Publisher

For Chris

Second Impression

Library of Congress Cataloging in Publication Data

Hoyt, Edwin Palmer.
African slavery.

Bibliography: p.
1. Slave trade—History. 2. Slavery in Africa.
3. Slavery in the United States. I. Title.
HT975.H68 382'.44'096 72–2079
ISBN 0–200–71899–1

NEW YORK
Abelard-Schuman
Limited
257 Park Avenue So.
10010

LONDON
Abelard-Schuman
Limited
450 Edgware Road W2 1EG

Published on the same day in Canada by Longman Canada Limited.

Printed in the United States of America
First published in Great Britain in 1974

Contents

Illustrations

1

The Early Days

Slavery has been the curse of every civilization at one time or another. In the period when man was a hunter, he did not enslave his male enemies, but killed them, and perhaps made off with their wives and children. These wives and children at first occupied a secondary place in the society they entered, but it was usually not long before they were fully integrated in the new tribe. So slavery, as such, did not really exist.

But when man settled down and began to work the land, he quickly discovered that if he could find cheap labor he could prosper. And he believed that slave labor was cheap, which it was, but only as long as human life was also cheap.

The ancients enslaved men. We know of slavery in the Fertile Crescent (Syria and Mesopotamia) and in ancient Egypt. The Greeks had slaves, both captives and persons born into slavery. The Romans built their empire on slavery and used slaves to build roads, harvest the crops, and serve in the Roman households. Some slaves in Rome rose to high position as gladiators, physicians, and even philosophers. But these were few when one considers the extent of slavery in ancient Rome. In the days of the Caesars, in the first 200 years after the birth of Christ, the slaves of Rome numbered some 20,000,000. Then the supply began to fall off with the end of the great Roman conquests, and by the fourth century a system of serfdom was growing up in Rome. The reason for it was the short supply of new slaves. The difference was that the serfs, or *coloni,* could go to court to secure remedy if their masters mistreated them, and the articles of their serfdom set down specific rules, such as those governing rent, which could not be changed. It was not freedom, but it was a long way from slavery, in which the master had the power of life or death over the slave.

Slavery in western Europe continued into the Middle Ages. The city-states that grew up in the wake of the Roman Empire dealt in slaves. The market for these Christian, European slaves, was the burgeoning Arab Empire, where men were wanted as soldiers and women were wanted for the harems.

There was, however, an important difference between the western concept of slavery and the Arab and African concept of slavery.

The western European tradition made the slave a piece of property: to be bought, thrust into the hold of a ship, fed slops, moved anywhere in the world, and then beaten and worked until he died. And the slave-owner needed to account to no one.

But the African tradition, which moved into the Arab world, was quite different. In the western European sense it was not even slavery, but a variety of patriarchism. A slave captured by one tribe from another came down in status, to be sure, but he had rights and was protected by the chief of the tribe to which he came. He was treated more as a junior member of the family than as an animal. It is a very great difference, and it must be acknowledged if one is to understand how the Africans allowed so many millions of their own people to be sold and sent across half the world. They could not conceive of the evil the white men would inflict upon these blacks, nor, living in a black society, could they conceive of the contempt in which the whites would hold the blacks.

To understand the blacks of Africa one must understand that Black Africa was never conquered from the outside until the nineteenth century. There had been many wars, but there were black kings fighting black kings in these struggles, and these kings were free, powerful, and even arrogant men. Indeed, a Catholic priest traveling in the Congo in 1687, wrote: "With nauseating presumption these nations think themselves the foremost men in the world and nothing will persuade them to the contrary. They imagine that Africa is not only the greatest part of the world, but also the happiest and most agreeable."

So it can be seen that the stereotype we have of

Slaves awaiting transport from East Africa

Africans as ignorant, foolish creatures who were easily enslaved is quite the wrong one. While Europe was growing into many kingdoms during the Middle Ages, so was Africa, in much the same way, although the two separate spheres knew nothing of one another. Africa had its feudal system, and if it was not just like Europe's variety, it was at least as enlightened—probably more so.

Contrary to popular thought, the slave trade did not start in the west of Africa and move into the New World. At least 1,000 years earlier, perhaps even around the beginning of the Christian era, it began in the east of Africa and moved north and northeast. The kings of East Africa were trading with the Mediterranean world by 60 A.D., and a guide to East African harbors drawn by an Egyptian Greek around that time still exists. Ships came from the Red Sea, the Persian Gulf, and from India and Ceylon to the African coast. Trading in goods was even older and can be generally traced back 2,000 years—although in the early years the trade was not for slaves.

By 800 A.D., there was a steady trade in slaves, probably due to the growth of the Arab Empire in the north and east. The Arabs of Mecca and Medina, who moved out to conquer the Arabian peninsula, were relatively few in number. Conquest and the taking of slaves, who were immediately converted to Islam, swelled the numbers. But this slavery was nothing like western slavery. An Arab slave was invariably well treated, and if he was abused his master had to account to the imam, a religious leader, and other Islamic authorities. If a free woman ever suckled a slave child, that child could never be sold by the family—he became in effect a member of the family.

By 957 A.D. when an Arab trading post was very active at Kilwa Kisiwani on the East African coast, the slave trade was well established, but it was a relatively gentle trade. Slaves were taken to the east—and there exists a report to the emperor of China in 1178 which discusses slaves and slave ships coming there from Africa.

One should not become too impressed with the humanity of these eastern slave-dealers, however, because fifty years later another Chinese scholar wrote about a sea disaster and told of slaves being used to stop up the leaks in the ship. That inhumanity reminds one of the treatment of slaves in the western sailing ships 600 years later.

Yet an important consideration is that while there were dozens of port cities up and down the eastern coast of Africa that traded with the outside world, slave-trading was only a small part of that commerce. The trade was in gold and ivory and incense *and slaves.* In China around the twelfth century three taels (about four ounces) of gold would buy a healthy slave. It would also buy a big bundle of aromatic wood.

There is another indication of the humanity of the slavers of the east, as compared to the west. Anyone traveling in the Arab world will note the darkness of skins and the African look about some people. This is an indication of the treatment of the slaves: intermarriage between Arabs and African slaves was quite acceptable. Another indication lies in the fact that there is nowhere in the eastern world a minority of Africans who have been downtrodden, the way there is in the United States. Modern authorities do not believe the eastern slave trade ever achieved the dimensions of the western trade, but that is not as important as the manner in which the people were treated during and after their enslavement. In the eastern world, the slaves were absorbed. In the western world, they were set apart.

One thing is certainly true about slavery in Africa: the modern tradition dates back to the voyage of Vasco da Gama, and the exploitation of Africa by the Portuguese. In 1502, da Gama, on his second voyage around Africa, subdued Kilwa, the great trade center. Two years later the Portuguese leader Almida sacked Kilwa and ruined its trade. Great and important places, such as Zanzibar and Mozambique, were turned into havens for the Portuguese trade in everything valuable, which included slaves. It took the western mentality, then, to take a trade that had been restrained, if valuable, and turn it into something quite different. As the Portuguese moved, and particularly after they conquered Brazil, they made the east coast of Africa a slaving center, with the slaves brought around the Cape of Good Hope to Rio de Janeiro and other ports. In some years 10,000 to 15,000 slaves were thus bought —not an important figure compared to perhaps five times as many in the West African trade. The trade did not move so quickly in the east of Africa. And even when it came, the Portuguese were not the only guilty ones. The French began slaving there, with Zanzibar as their principal port, when they settled Mauritius and Bourbon. The Sultan of Oman made slaving a major business, and at the time that slavers from the west were operating on the rivers of the Gold Coast, the Arabs were penetrating Africa from the east and bringing out thousands of slaves. It is said that it was not until 1852 when slavers from the east first encountered slavers from the west in the center of Africa.

2

The Europeans Come

By the fifteenth century, the people of the interior of Africa were embarking on a new period, in which the tides of rule were changing. Kingdoms were at constant war with each other, and in these wars they took captives, who became slaves in the African sense—vassals, or people owing allegiance to their masters. They were restricted in seeking wives and in their occupations, but they were still members of the society, and no African thought of his fellow African as potential *property.*

The rulers, such as the Hausa of northern Nigeria, would set up an oligarchy of nobles who controlled the kingdom, and this oligarchy in time would control the lives of the common people. The people could be called to labor in the fields for their masters, to build houses for them, or to maintain the roads. In some places, such as East Africa, literally no one was *free,* because the social structure was so tightly interwoven. In Rwanda,

Slaves being brought from the deep interior of Africa

for example, the society was divided into three parts. First came the Watusi, who did not work but fought the wars. Second came the Bahutu, who managed affairs, and did the work we could today ascribe to the middle class. Third came the Batwa, pygmies who had been conquered in war, and performed the more menial tasks. But even the Watusi considered themselves to be the vassals of their chiefs. Slavery as we of the west know it, did exist, in such places as the Ugandan kingdom of Ankole, but it was not very common. Slaveholding was restricted to the very rich, and the number of slaves was limited.

Thus, a slave might be in almost any walk of life. Indeed, kings of the interior sometimes sent slaves as heads of caravans to trade with the coast. When they arrived at the coast, they had complete power to represent their masters and were trusted as much as any other emissaries. And sometimes these slaves acquired slaves. One can see that this system, using the word and concept of slave but not the western meaning at all, was totally misunderstood by the first Europeans who visited Africa. An African slave of the Ashanti tribe might marry, own property, own a slave, swear an oath, and even inherit his master's property. This is an attitude toward slavery few westerners can understand.

The meeting of the two cultures began in 1441, some fifty years before Columbus crossed the Atlantic in search of the Indies. In 1441 a young Portuguese captain named Antam Gonçalvez sailed out from his homeland, bound for the rocky coast of Africa, to capture sea lions. A few years earlier some storm-driven sea captain had discovered a sea lion colony, killed some of the beasts, and brought their hides and oil home to Portugal. The discovery had created a sensation, and now the search for sea lions was on.

Gonçalvez took his little sailing ship to the south of what is now Morocco, and the Spanish colony Río de Oro. It was a valiant achievement; sailing down the coast was easy enough because the wind blew from the north toward the south, but sailing back he would have to tack constantly, sailing against the wind. He was able to maneuver this way, where Portuguese ships had not done it before, because the Portuguese had just begun to use the fore-and-aft sail used in the Mediterranean. This sail hung on a line with the ship, as opposed to the square sails, which were suspended athwartships in back of the masts. So with the fore-and-aft sails, the little ship could sail much more closely into the wind than under the old system.

One can see that someone back in Portugal was very adventurous, and this was true: he was Prince Henry the Navigator, the ruler of Portugal, and he was very much interested in foreign lands. Gonçalvez knew his ruler, and he decided to bring home some captives from Africa to exhibit at court and thus win acclaim for himself. With nine of his men he went ashore one night and captured a dark-skinned man and a dark-skinned woman and took them home to Lisbon.

Gonçalvez was followed by other adventurers. One of his lieutenants captured a black man of royal birth.

This captive was very intelligent and knowledgeable about his world and excited Prince Henry to the point that he decided to conquer the territory for Portugal. Now, in those days, the help or hindrance of the Pope was all-important, so Henry sent an emissary to the Pope describing his plan and received the papal blessing in the interest of extending Christianity to Africa. That, of course, was not Henry's motive at all.

It is said that this black noble persuaded Gonçalvez to take him home on his next voyage, with the promise that he would give him in exchange several other "Black Moors." Gonçalvez did so and received some ten blacks from various countries. These were captives of the Berber tribe from which the captive noble had come.

Now began the slaving. Nuño Tristão, one of Gonçalvez's men, went to Africa in 1443 and captured twenty-nine blacks from canoes in which they were paddling offshore. In a few months another slaver went south and came home with 235 captives. And then the slaving began in earnest, with whole squadrons of caravels sailing south, surprising villages, and enslaving the people they found there—men, women, and children.

Discovering the Portuguese market for slaves, the Berbers began making trips inland and buying slaves from the kings of the interior, in exchange for horses, Spanish silk, silver, and other valuables. Thus, by force and by trade, the western slave trade began—many, many years after the eastern trade. And the Berbers, who had seen the lives of slaves in the Arab world, might well have expected the western Europeans to treat their slaves in the same way.

In the beginning the Portuguese slave trade was a royal concession, and it continued that way for the first fifty years. In those years the trade from Africa tripled, and by 1500, some 3,500 Africans each year were being shipped to Europe, where almost all of them remained in Portugal and Spain, since other European countries had no use for slaves.

For that reason, when Captain William Hawkins made the first English voyage to Africa in 1530, he brought back a cargo of ivory, but no slaves. The English captains were offered slaves but they refused them; they were showing very good profits by dealing in merchandise alone.

Around 1560 Queen Elizabeth of England became interested in what was called the Guinea trade and sent her ships to Africa to secure ivory and pepper, in particular. At least one of these voyages produced a profit of ten times the capital risked, and word spread very rapidly that the African trade was something to be watched. In another ten years the French were engaged in the African trade—but the French, too, vowed that they would not deal in human flesh.

What then changed the minds of all these high-minded Europeans who would not buy slaves? Nothing more nor less than the discovery of America.

3

Slaves to America

Everything changed when Christopher Columbus sailed to the island now shared by the governments of Haiti and the Dominican Republic. In 1493, the "discovery" of the "New World" brought about an immediate change in the Americas, Europe, and Africa. Within a few years after Columbus's voyage, the Spanish conquistadores were using the local Indians of their conquered territories as slaves. The Spanish historian Antonio Herrera de Tordesillas reported that in 1495 Columbus put down an insurrection of natives on Hispaniola (now called Santo Domingo). These Indians had rebelled against being enslaved, and thousands of them were massacred by the Spanish troops. Thousands more were put to work in the mines and fields.

As Spanish rule expanded in South America and the southern portion of North America, the Spanish enslaved the Indians as they went along. In Mexico the slaves were sent to mine gold and silver. In Peru they mined gold and silver and emeralds for Francisco Pizarro's men.

But the people of the Americas were not "good slaves." Many died from harsh treatment and disease, and others died because they lost the will to live. The Spanish governors then sent home for slaves and indentured servants to take the place of the Indians. But by 1503, they saw this system working very badly: that year the governor of Hispaniola complained to the court at home that fugitive black slaves were teaching disobedience and committing acts of violence in the mines and elsewhere. He asked for an end to the export of black slaves because they were too hard to handle, and Queen Isabella acceded. Only white slaves were exported then, most of them captured from Europe or European vessels, and many of them were women who were placed in brothels.

But the pressures were too great. By 1510, the same governor of Hispaniola had changed his mind and was asking for blacks. The natives were dying too rapidly, and Africans were now brought to the New World for sale.

So serious did the matter of dying slaves become that in 1517 a Spanish priest named Bartolomé de las Casas went back to Spain, after seeing conditions in the New World, to intercede with King Charles V in behalf of the Indians. He told the king's courtiers that he had a solution to the vexing problem. During his stay in the Americas, Padre Bartolomé had seen Africans brought to the West Indies and the mainland in Spanish ships. These blacks adjusted very well to the food and climate of the Indians and seemed to be able to work longer and harder than the native Americans. Padre Bartolomé's idea was to substitute black slavery for Indian slavery. The courtiers listened, and Padre Bartolomé had his audience with the king. The result was that Spain became officially involved in the slave trade of the western world when King Charles granted a permit *(asiento)* to one of his courtiers to take 4,000 African slaves to the West Indies. It was the year of Padre Bartolomé's visit home, 1517.

The priest was not very accurate in his estimate that the character of the blacks was docile. The Africans kidnapped and taken to the New World rebelled. In 1522 a group rose in rebellion in Hispaniola. In 1527 another group rebelled in Puerto Rico. In 1529 a third group fought for their lives in Santa Marta, and two years later a fourth uprising occurred in Panama. So serious were these that the Spanish developed a special police force in the New World for chasing runaway slaves.

And yet the profits derived from slavery were such that the unruly slaves did not discourage the slaveholders. There was too much money to be made in the trade and too much need for cheap labor in the new land.

At about this same time, Brazil was being settled by the Portuguese, whose navigators had first sighted the coast in 1500. The Portuguese established slave trading posts on the shores of West Africa, and the Spanish were not far behind. When the word spread through Europe about this new trade, businessmen in other countries became interested. For the next 200 years Spain, Portugal, England, France, the Netherlands, Germany, and Sweden would quarrel over the profitable slave trade, but the Spanish and Portuguese would always be the leaders. The very word "Negro" is from the Spanish and Portuguese words for black. Many words were similarly adopted, such as: *barracoon,* which means the stockade in which the slaves were penned after they were captured and before they were sold to the ship captains; *palaver,* to talk; *pickaninny,* which comes from *pequeñino;* and *fetish,* which comes from the Portuguese *feitico,* meaning charm.

The Spanish and the Portuguese began the western slave trade, but the English were soon giving them strong competition. One of the first English slavers was Captain John Hawkins. Hawkins was a seafarer and the son of William Hawkins who had been involved in the Guinea trade years earlier, but only for ivory and spices. But young Hawkins was more ambitious, and he decided to go into the trade in human flesh. He secured the backing of London merchants who supplied him with three ships: the *Salomon,* the *Swallow,* and the *Jonas.* With a hundred men, he left England in October, 1562, and went to Guinea. There he secured slaves by the easiest, if most dangerous, means of all—he attacked Portuguese slave ships. From one Portuguese slaver he seized 200 blacks, from three others he took 70 each, and from a fifth he took 500—or so the Portuguese complained. It was doubtful if Hawkins could have taken so many in his small ships.

Hawkins took his slaves to Hispaniola where he traded them for hides, sugar, spices, and Peruvian emeralds. Queen Elizabeth I of England first called Hawkins's voyage "detestable," but when she learned how profitable it had been, the queen became a shareholder in the Hawkins business. (Hawkins also introduced a young captain named Francis Drake into the slave trade.) So now, with the coming of the English into the trade, the competition grew.

The first slave ship to come to the coast of North America was a Dutch galleon, which arrived off Jamestown, Virginia, in August, 1619, to trade with the colonies. Her captain brought merchandise from Europe and twenty African slaves who were sold to the English. Colonist John Rolfe, who married the Indian princess Pocahontas, recorded the coming of the ship, although he did not state her name.

That same year, the earl of Warwick and his representative in Virginia, Captain Samuel Argall, outfitted a privateer, or private military vessel, to which the Crown gave a commission to fight against the Spaniards. But the captain of the ship quickly learned there was more money to be made in selling African slaves to Virginians than in risking his neck against the Spaniards, so he stopped raiding Spanish vessels and began trading with the Spanish instead. His ship, the *Treasurer,* might be considered the first American slave ship, although she traded only in the Western Hemisphere.

Inspection and sale of an African

The *Treasurer* plied between the American Atlantic coast and the Spanish colonies of the West Indies for a number of years until she became unseaworthy and was destroyed in Bermuda.

It did not take long for the English colonists to take up slave-trading. Soon the Massachusetts colony was sending ships to the West Indies, and these ships were bringing back slaves as well as sugar and molasses. One of the first of these ships was the *Desire,* which sailed from Marblehead, Massachusetts, in 1636, on a trading voyage, and after seven months brought back a cargo of slaves. To Virginia belongs the questionable honor of having brought the first American slaves direct from Africa, rather than by way of the Indies. The ship *Fortune* captured a Portuguese vessel loaded with slaves off the African coast and brought them to Virginia, where the captain traded the slaves for a cargo of tobacco.

In the seventeenth century the English were at almost constant war with the Spanish and the Portuguese, and any cargoes the privateers captured were welcome to the men who backed these irregular war vessels. But in this same period the English colonists learned how and where the Spanish and Portuguese got their slaves and began going to the source, Africa's west coast.

One might stop for a moment and ponder how the English, in particular, could justify slavery. The fact is that slavery was not such a far step for the English, and other North Europeans, even in the seventeenth century. For more than two hundred years it had been the practice in Europe for poor people who had no hope of achieving success to sign papers of indenture, or voluntary slavery, usually for a period of five to ten years. These indentured servants would be cared for and perhaps even educated by their masters as long as they worked faithfully. Many people came to the New World, and particularly to the English and Dutch colonies, as indentured servants.

The system of indenture did not work very well, however, because the servants were always being replaced. The term would run out, and the "servant" would become a freedman who had to be paid off and given land of his own. So the Dutch in the seventeenth century began to bring African slaves to Nieuw Amsterdam, and soon there were blacks all along the Dutch shores of the Hudson River, as far upstream as Albany. In spite of this movement, slavery did not flourish in the cold colonies of the north, where the lands were rocky and farms tended to be small. But in the West Indies and southern lands of North America, the plantation owners had thousands of acres to plant with cotton and sugar and tobacco. They needed cheap labor to tend these crops, and the slaves provided that cheap labor.

In 1663 the Royal African Company was chartered by the British Crown and backed by Parliament. Before the beginning of the next century the British were also transporting slaves to the Spanish colonies under a treaty with Spain, which called for the Spanish to take 4,800 black slaves a year for thirty years from British traders.

By then slaving had grown to be a very big business. The Royal African Company alone had 249 slave ships. It was estimated that from 1600 to 1700 an average of 27,500 slaves each year were shipped from Guinea to the New World, which meant that in one century some 2,750,000 blacks were brought to the Americas and the West Indies. Of course, not all these slaves survived, but thousands had been shipped before and hundreds of thousands would be shipped afterward. The whites were creating a large black population in the Western Hemisphere.

In the beginning, the slaves seem to have been treated fairly well, because there were so few of them. But as more blacks came to the New World and were easily bought and sold, the whites began to show a contempt for the slaves and to regard them as no better than animals. But there was another powerful reason for the mistreatment of slaves in the New World. It was fear.

By the end of the seventeenth century, the whites had brought so many slaves west that in some places the blacks outnumbered the whites. For example, Barbados, an island in the West Indies, had 46,000 black slaves and 20,000 white masters. In Jamaica, the blacks outnumbered the whites ten to one. These two islands were noted for the cruelty practiced against the slaves as the whites struggled to maintain control.

The slaves were punished in any manner that their masters saw fit to use, and no law protected the blacks from any cruelties. For serious crimes, slaves were nailed to the ground by sticks thrust through their hands and feet, and then burned almost to death. For lesser crimes, a slave might be lashed, or half of one foot might be cut off. A slave who ran away and was caught was usually forced to wear heavy rings around his legs thereafter. A cruel master might pour salt and pepper into his wounds to hurt him more. All through the centuries, particularly in the West Indies, there had been serious slave uprisings, and it was because of this fear of rebellion that the planters and slave-traders reigned with whip and iron over their blacks.

4

The American Slave Trade

Before 1700 there were slaves in every American colony, although in the area above Chesapeake Bay the slaves were usually household servants of the rich. In 1700 there were even 1,000 blacks in New England, and in 1715, it was reported that there were 2,000 blacks in Boston alone. The slave trade brought more Africans each year, and when the first American census was taken in 1790, the slave population was shown to be 697,000 of a total population of 3,930,000, or approximately 18 percent.

In the eighteenth century, slave-trading took hold in New England, with the development of what was called the "triangular trade," which, in turn, depended on the economic relationships of England and her colonies. Sugar was grown in the West Indies, and the New Englanders discovered that they had the resources and ability to make the sugar into rum. Sea captains, then,

Slaves cultivating sugarcane in the West Indies

set out with rum to trade. But who would buy rum? The African chiefs of West Africa would buy great quantities of rum and pay for it in slaves. The planters of the Indies wanted slaves. So the New England ship captains sold their rum to the West Africans, bought slaves, and took them to the West Indies, where they were paid in sugar and molasses, which New England distilleries made into rum. The central port for the slave-traders was Newport, Rhode Island.

Newport was the home of Captain David Lindsay, one of the most notorious of the Yankee slave-traders of the eighteenth century. By the middle of the century, Lindsay owned and commanded the brigantine *Sanderson,* a 40-ton ship, about ten years old. (Indeed, after the first years of the African trade, the buying and selling of slaves tended to fall into the hands of such captains who would risk much for a quick profit. In these years, of course, slave-trading was a perfectly legitimate business in America and England. The dangers were disease, piracy, and possible capture by enemies.) In 1752 Lindsay decided he would sell the *Sanderson* and buy a bigger vessel for the slave trade. He found no immediate takers for the *Sanderson,* so he sailed in her once again to the West Indies for a cargo of molasses. Then Lindsay made still another voyage, this time to Africa.

Early in 1753 the ship was off the African coast, trading rum, old muskets, and cloth for slaves. Captain Lindsay was encountering the major difficulty of the trade: sickness. His first and second mates, and three men of the crew were sick and confined to their quarters. Probably they had malaria, which was prevalent on that coast in those days.

Lindsay was a daring man, but he was growing restless. In a letter home, he complained that he still had thirteen or fourteen hogsheads of rum to trade, but that the trade was going so slowly that he was nearly frantic. His anchor cable was worn through, and he had been forced to buy another. He was worried about his ship and did not believe she would hold up much longer, for he could see daylight around her bow beneath the deck, which meant that the timbers were separating.

The captain finally set sail from the Guinea coast with fifty-six slaves aboard and managed to reach Barbados safely. The voyage took him ten weeks, of which twenty-two days were rainy and stormy, so rough that the wind beat his sails to pieces and several times they had to be taken down for mending. Of the fifty-six slaves, he lost only one girl on the voyage, and he boasted that the others had arrived healthy and "fatt."

Not all the captains of the slave trade were as fortunate or perhaps as thoughtful as Captain Lindsay, however. Captain Collingwood of the *Zong* threw a cargo of 130 slaves overboard because they were diseased, and he figured that he could make more profit by collecting the insurance than by selling the unfit slaves in the western colonies.

Yes, the slave trade was extremely profitable, as the career of Captain William Boates showed. Boates was found a few hours after his birth drifting in a boat in

Liverpool harbor. He was raised in an orphanage, and while still a boy was apprenticed to a shipmaster. He went from the job of cabin boy to that of seaman, and in a few years had managed to become captain of his own ship. In January, 1758, he was captain of the *Knight,* which sailed from the Guinea coast with 398 slaves aboard. Six weeks later he landed at Jamaica and unloaded 360 slaves. Then off the Leeward Islands, his ship was attacked by a French privateer, which attempted to sink the *Knight.* When that attempt failed, the French tried to board the English ship, but Captain Boates and his men drove off the Frenchmen in a fierce battle. After many such adventures, in which he acquired the nickname "Billy" among the slavers, Boates saved enough money to give up the slave trade and become a banker. Then he sent slave ships to sea—dozens of them—and he reaped the profits of the trade. He died in England a very wealthy man.

As such men in England and the West Indies grew rich from trading in human flesh, the Americans were not far behind. But there was a difference: the slaves came to the West Indies and the Americas and became part of the culture. Slavery was made more palatable, in the American colonies, too, because the colonial governments taxed slaveowners on the basis of the number of slaves they owned. Massachusetts, New York, and Rhode Island all secured money by taxing slaveowners for revenue. Only New Jersey, among all the colonies, taxed slavery in order to destroy the practice. Other colonials said New Jersey did so to protect the importation of indentured white servants. Pennsylvania, peopled by Quakers who opposed slavery in principle, was the first colony to place a really prohibitive tax of twenty English pounds per head on slaves. Shortly before the American Revolution, North Carolina placed a forty-pound tax on *imported* slaves, because the number of blacks in the colony had grown so large that many whites were afraid of a slave uprising. From time to time these taxes were raised or lowered, but gradually it became apparent that slavery was acceptable to the majority of the whites, particularly in the southern colonies.

When the Declaration of Independence was signed in 1776, slavery was legal in all of the thirteen original colonies. After the revolution, as the states drew up their constitutions, in the 1780's, the northern states began to outlaw slavery, as well as the slave trade. By 1800, the conflict between North and South over slavery became a serious national problem. One of the causes of this growing conflict was an invention, the cotton gin, perfected by Eli Whitney in 1793. Before the cotton gin, in 1792, the southern states had exported 138,000 pounds of cotton. In 1800, after the gin came into general use in the South, the cotton states exported 17,790,000 pounds of cotton. The gin cleaned the cotton of seeds and leaves, but someone still had to pick the cotton bolls. The planters used slaves even more for cheap labor.

Particularly in the North, there was much agitation against the continuation of the slave trade, and actually most states had outlawed the trade by 1800. Slave importation was legal only in Georgia and South Carolina. The New England states, where most of the slave-traders lived, had specifically forbidden their citizens to engage in the slave trade. But the laws were constantly flouted, and the number of American slave-traders on the coasts of Africa increased every year. The demand for slaves grew so great after 1800 that Charleston, South Carolina, was the leading slave port in America and one of the most important slave ports in the world. Between 1804 and 1807 more than 200 ships landed slave cargoes in that city, and in the year 1807 alone more than 15,000 slaves were landed there.

In 1808 Congress abolished the slave trade in all the United States, but that did not mean very much. Illegal slave-trading continued and flourished, until President Jefferson stopped all American ships from sailing for Europe with his embargo of 1807 and 1808. Jefferson's embargo was levied because of a general quarrel with England over shipping rights, tariffs, and the impressment of American seamen into the British Navy. These issues had little to do with the slave trade directly, but the embargo slowed the trade. The War of 1812 put an end to almost all foreign trade, but not to the slave trade. Spanish ships could sail easily from Cuba to the ports of the South, and, if necessary, conceal themselves along the rivers. The end of the War of 1812 found Savannah, Georgia, and New Orleans, Louisiana, becoming the most important American slaving ports.

5

Tales of the Slave Coast—I

The area of Africa called the Slave Coast lay on the western side of the continent, between the Senegal River and the Congo River, encompassing a long expanse of sea coast, including the rounding bottom of the great bulge of the African shoreline. This coast was mostly flat; parts of it were covered by sandy beaches; other parts, by swamp and jungle to the water's edge. It was steamy and marshy and dangerous to ships, for much of the water was too shallow for oceangoing vessels, and there were few good harbors.

The slave ships would come in near the shore and anchor inside the sandbars at the mouth of one of the larger rivers, then send their boats ashore. That was the best and safest way for the traders. But sometimes the slave-traders would go to a point where there was no river and no protective sandbar. Then they had to anchor offshore, while the ship's boats and African canoes moved back and forth in shark-filled waters that were notable for dangerous tides and surf that rolled and pounded against the shore.

There were a hundred places where slaves might be bought along this coast. In the beginning, when the Portuguese and Spanish began to develop the trade, the slave vessels came into African waters and their captains went ashore to bargain for slaves by ones and twos. These were slaves in the old African tradition—captives of wars and raids, who had been enslaved by the victors and were being passed on to the whites for gold or cloth or tools. As time went on, the trade became heavily concentrated in certain sure-fire areas along the western bulge of Africa. One such area was the Grain Coast, which extended from Cape Mount to Cape Palmas. The second part was the Ivory Coast, which extended from Cape Palmas to the Lagos River. Next to the Ivory Coast lay the Gold Coast, which extended down to the Volta River. Then came the Bight of Benin, the section of the coast that curves back in from the bulge, and here lay the Slave Coast itself. On these coasts the English and the Portuguese and other slaving nations came and built forts. The most important of the English forts was Cape Coast Castle, which guarded the Gold Coast of the Ashanti and Fan country. Not far away was a Dutch fort, and near that was a Danish fort.

East of the Cape Coast Castle lay Anamboe, the port where Captain David Lindsay of Newport had called on his slaving voyages. In its day Anamboe was the major port of embarkation for the American slave trade. But by the end of the first half of the eighteenth century its importance had fallen off, and Accra was taking over. The people in Accra were warlike and usually had prisoners to sell to the whites. To be able to gather a shipload of slaves in a week or two was a great accomplishment in the early days of slaving. It meant that the white captain and crew would be subjected that much less to the dangers of the fevers that swept this area. So Accra in 1800 was a favorite port and was much frequented by the white slavers.

The Slave Coast was the most profitable of all in terms of trade. Costs were lower there, and slaves could be rounded up quickly. But the Slave Coast was also the most dangerous of all coasts to visit. The country was flat, and the surf was more vicious than anywhere else. Between April and July that surf ran so high that many natives would not venture out into it. Anyone who could take a boat through the breakers must have two lives, they said. But here the king of Dahomey had enslaved all the coastal tribes, and many slaves were to be found. Spurred by the prospects of high profit, the slave ships came in, braving the dangers of surf and sharks. Along the whole of this coast there was not a single navigable stream between the Sherboro River, south of Sierra Leone, for 1,500 miles to the Benin River. In the bight at Calabar, on the Bonny River, were good pickings for the slavers, and for years the white slavers met the black slavers who came down the river in their canoes, carrying human cargo. During the years when the English were leading the slave trade, 12,000 to 15,000 slaves a year were picked up here.

Spanish, Portuguese, and other traders continued in the business of enslaving Africans during the whole life of the trade, which did not end until the United States outlawed slavery in the 1860's. But beginning in the eighteenth century, London, the headquarters of the Royal African Company, was one center of the trade. Bristol was another. Liverpool got into the trade, too, and came to dominate the slave trade after the middle of the century. In 1764 Bristol had thirty-two ships in the trade, and Liverpool had seventy-four. Seven years later Liverpool claimed 107 and by the end of the century a quarter of all Liverpool's ships were engaged in the slave trade, which meant that she had three-sevenths of all the European African trade, and that her only serious rival was the city of Newport, Rhode Island.

In England in these times, a man could live well on thirty English pounds a year. At the height of the trade, the Liverpool merchants were selling more than a million pounds worth of slaves each year in the Americas. Many an English and American shipping fortune was based on the trade in human flesh, and this money was reinvested in other businesses and created more wealth. Indeed, one student of capitalism, Eric Williams, wrote in his book *Capitalism and Slavery* (1944), that the slave trade was responsible for the speed of development of the Industrial Revolution because it supplied the capital for canals, railroads, and even the steam engine.

As the English gained dominance on the Guinea coast, the manner of slave-trading began to change. Slaving was as much adventure as business, as a letter from Captain John Griffen at Anamboe on the African coast indicates. Captain Griffen was writing home to his backer.

After paying his respects he blessed God that he had his health, but said he expected a long and troublesome journey. He said there had "never been so much rum on the coast at one time before"—which meant so many American slave-traders, who dealt largely in rum. Nor had he seen so many Frenchmen before; it was almost eerie, there were so many French ships. The captain could not give an estimate as to when he might get away from the coast with his load of slaves. He explained to his backer that in several weeks of waiting he had been able to buy only twenty-seven slaves because there were so many ships in the roads. Looking out around him he counted nineteen ships that day. Slaves were very scarce, he said, and those ships that he knew by reputation as carrying only "prime slaves" were forced to take any that came along this year. The captain recounted other woes typical of the slave trade: he had lost his first mate to fever a few days earlier, and another member of the crew as well. Two of the slaves he had managed to buy had somehow escaped him and had gone overboard, preferring to face the sharks rather than stay in bondage.

Africans being pursued by slavers

This letter was written hastily, for obviously it was to be entrusted to some other slave ship which was going to sea immediately, having loaded its cargo. It was written at a time when the slave trade was in a period of change. The European forts were still dominating the trade in the days of John Griffen, but their days were numbered. As the more powerful African tribes were corrupted into securing slaves for the trade, the forts became unnecessary. The African slave-traders did much of the capturing.

An Englishman who went up the Niger River witnessed a slave raiding party at work while traveling near the confluence of the Niger and the Tschadda rivers, in the territory of the Felatah tribe. The Englishman reported:

> Scarcely a night passed but we heard the screams of some unfortunate beings that were carried off into slavery by these villainous depredators [the African native slavers]. The inhabitants of the towns in the route of the Felatahs fled across the river on the approach of the enemy. A few days after the arrival of the fugitives [who were escaping] a column of smoke rising in the air, about five miles above the confluence marked the advance of the Felatahs; and in two days afterwards the whole of the towns, including Addah Cuddah, and five or six others, were in a blaze. The shrieks of the unfortunate wretches that had not escaped, answered by the loud wailings and lamentations of

their friends and relations at seeing them carried off into slavery, and their habitations destroyed, produced a scene, which, though common enough in the country, had seldom, if ever before, been witnessed by European eyes, and showed to me, in a more striking light than I had hitherto beheld it, the horrors attendant upon slavery.

Aside from capture in war or raid, there were several other ways that an African might be made a slave. A debtor could be enslaved and sold. A tribesman who took another man's wife could be enslaved. An African who disturbed another's *fetish,* or religious symbol, might be enslaved. And in some tribes a man might sell his wives and children into slavery. In the most corrupt tribes the chiefs sometimes sent their wives out to trap lovers, who were then enslaved. They persuaded witch doctors to fabricate charges against strong young men, so they might be sold. It was common for a chief to declare a war just to bring in slaves.

As the demand for slaves grew, the chiefs and kings lost their monopoly of the slave business in Africa. Ordinary tribesmen began delivering captives to the ships. One practice was simple kidnapping. The tribesmen would lie in wait and snatch a passerby in the jungle, then sell him into slavery. Alexander Falconbridge, an Englishman who served as a doctor on a slave ship, told how one woman went to visit a neighbor one evening on invitation. The moment the visitor entered her friend's hut, she was set upon by two men who bound

Stowing slave cargo at night

her and took her aboard a ship and then sold her to the captain. A native from the interior was promised a free drink of rum if he would accompany another tribesman to a ship. He went and, once aboard, discovered that his "friend" had sold him into slavery.

Soon the Africans along the west coast found they could trust practically no one. An English sailor saw a dealer bring a slave to his ship and then paddle his canoe back through the surf to shore. As the sailor watched, four men jumped on the slave-seller, bound him, and then brought him out to the ship to become a slave.

Some Africans along the coast became noted as slavers. One of these was called Ben Johnson by the whites. One day Ben Johnson came aboard a ship bringing a girl he had captured, or kidnapped. Johnson left the ship, and then two other Africans came aboard and asked about the girl, for they were her relatives. The captain told them that he had just bought her from Johnson, whereupon the two men rushed from the ship and back to shore. They found Ben Johnson, surprised him and bound him, and then delivered him and sold him as a slave to the captain who had bought the girl.

These two men accepted the unwritten law of the coast, that a slave sale was a sale and not to be argued, but the slaves did not accept their captivity so easily. In the early days of slave-trading the new slaves were put aboard the ships as soon as they were brought to the coast and kept aboard ship until the captain was ready to sail. When a captain arrived in African waters, he would strike the yards and topmasts of the ship and lash the yards from mast to mast a few feet above the deck to build a ridgepole. Other spars were fixed from this to the standing rigging of the ship, and a lattice work was built across this framework. This was covered with fibers and mats to keep out the rain. A plank division was then built across the ship near the mainmast, extending out about two feet on each side of the vessel, about eight feet tall. A door was cut in this *barricado,* and a sentry stood at the door. This division separated the slaves—men from women—so they could all be kept on deck while the slave ship was loading.

As the demand grew, the African traders became more aggressive, too. At Bonny, for example, a group of black traders would load twenty or thirty canoes with trade goods and then go upriver. They would come back without goods, but with the canoes loaded with slaves, who were then sold to the white ship captains and put aboard the slave ship.

6

Tales of the Slave Coast—II

Another way that blacks were obtained was by the process called *buckra panyaring,* or mass kidnapping. A famous instance of this occurred at the mouth of the Old Calabar River in 1767.

On one side of this river lived the king of Old Town with his tribe, and on the other side lived the king of New Town. Both kings had become wealthy in the slave trade, and they were bitter rivals, sending their canoes upcountry as far as a hundred miles where they traded for some slaves and kidnapped others. Together, the two towns were said to provide some 7,000 slaves a year to the white traders.

Each of these kings thought life would be much better if his rival were eliminated, and they struggled so hard for power that in 1767 the whole slave trade of the region was brought to a halt because neither king dared to send his warriors up the river in case the other king should attack his town while his warriors were away. One ship after another came to the mouth of the river, and there it sat, until there were seven English ships at anchor, and seven restless English captains grumbling day and night.

One night six of these captains met and agreed to bring this unpleasant situation to an end by siding with the New Town king. They informed him of their decision, and the next day the captains invited the people of both towns to come to the ships for rum and brandy. The Old Towners came out in force, and the king of New Town sent enough of his people to allay the suspicions of the others. The rum and brandy were broken out, and the Africans caroused all day and all night.

At eight o'clock the next morning, one of the captains ordered a gun fired. This was the agreed-upon signal. The ships' crews came charging forward, clubbing the Old Towners who were still on the vessels, the New Towners having quietly gotten away. Many Old Towners jumped overboard, but the ships' crews sank their canoes with gunfire, and those who escaped were forced to swim for their lives.

The New Towners came down to the shores to wait for the escaping Old Towners. They were supposed to capture them as slaves, but their bloodlust was aroused, and they killed as many as they captured. The king of Old Town, a big, strong man, was set upon by New Towners, but escaped to the safety of his palace. His three brothers were captured, and two of them were sold into slavery. The other was killed by the New Towners.

When the slaughter was over, it was estimated that 300 blacks of Old Town had died, and an equal number had been captured. The Englishmen sailed away with them as slaves, but that was not the end of the war. Next year, as an English ship lay in the harbor, the Old Town people attacked New Town, and dealt with the inhabitants in the same fashion.

As the demand for slaves grew, other methods were used by the white slave-traders. They sometimes accompanied the black slavers inland and gave large gifts to kings and tribal chiefs of the countryside, encouraging them to kidnap and make war on neighbors even farther inland, to meet the demand for slaves. Some captains adopted a practice called "pawning." They came to a coastal town and offered the king a large sum for a shipload of slaves. But to secure the bargain, they demanded that "pawns," or members of the king's own tribe, be put aboard the ship as security. Then, if the slaves were not delivered, the ship captains threatened to sail away with the pawns. Some captains disagreed with this practice, because they said it destroyed relations with the coastal kings. They were proved right one day when an English slave ship captain on the Gambia River sailed off with a load of pawns, taking advantage of a favorable wind. The wind shifted, the ship was forced back, and the native king attacked the vessel, rescuing the pawns, killing the captain and all the crew, except one white boy, who was enslaved by the king and kept for several years until other white men arranged his release.

One black slave-trader was a Fula tribesman named

Job, a young man whose father was wealthy herdsman in the valley of the Senegal River. Job came down country to sell two slaves, moving down his own bank of the Gambia River, cautioned not to go to the other side where the Mandingos lived, for they might capture him and sell him into slavery. Job sold his slaves, then crossed the Gambia to buy some cattle, and, sitting at a feast with his weapons away from his side, he was set upon and captured by Mandingo slave-hunters, just as his father had warned him he might be. The Mandingos took Job to the king of the tribe, who sold the young man to the captain of the slave ship *Arabella,* receiving a pistol in return. The king was so pleased with the pistol that he put it on a cord around his neck and wore it day and night.

Job was taken across the Atlantic and eventually to Maryland where he became the property of a tobacco planter. The planter learned that Job was actually named Job ibn Solomon and that he was a devout Muslim. For a time Job worked in the fields with a hoe. Then the planter learned that he was a herdsman and put him to work with the cattle on the plantation. Given more freedom, Job ran away. He was captured and put in jail to await punishment by his master, who was notified and told to reclaim his "property."

While in jail, Job wrote a letter in Arabic, which was sent to England since nobody in Maryland could translate it, and finally to Oxford University, where a translator was found. The news of the remarkable letter and remarkable slave reached James Oglethorpe, an official of the Royal African Company, who was so impressed that he purchased Job from his Maryland master and had him brought to England.

In England it was discovered that Job ibn Solomon was an Arabic scholar. He was put to work translating Arabic documents into the English he had now learned. He also wrote out three copies of the Koran from memory. Soon he was taken under the protection of the duke of Montagu and was presented at the English court.

When Job was asked what he wanted from life, he said he wanted to go home, and his influential new friends finally sent him back to Africa. There, he arrived at the mouth of the Gambia River and began making his way upstream. At the village of Damasena he came upon some Mandingo tribesmen. He spoke with the men and learned that the old king of the Mandingos, who had sold Job into slavery, was dead. The pistol he always wore around his neck had discharged one day by accident and shot him through the throat. Job threw himself on the ground when he heard this news and gave thanks to Allah for making the king die by the gun he had received for Job's enslavement.

This was one slave's story with a happy ending: Job went home and settled down to live among his people again.

But there were very few such tales in the slave trade, and as the need for slaves in the west grew stronger, the slavers became more callous in their treatment of the blacks.

As the eighteenth century wore on and the forts became less important, they were turned into trading posts, which were operated by *factors,* or representatives from the European countries. Soon these installations became know as "factories." The factors lived on the coast, under the protection of the Europeans and the native kings, with whom they had made slaving arrangements. A factory was surrounded by a stockade and perhaps even by a moat. The factor built a *barracoon* inside, and he hired a guard of African mercenaries that was armed with muskets and swords. The *barracoons* were made of heavy piles driven into the earth and lashed together with bamboo. The top was thatched with palm leaves. In the center of the barracoon was a row of piles, and a chain extended along each line of piles. Every two or three feet a neckline was put in the chain, to hold male slaves. The walls of the barracoon rose four to six feet high, and then there was an opening of about four feet all around, to allow for the circulation of air beneath the roof.

These airy barracoons were built to avoid having the slaves sicken and die before they could be moved away from the hot and dangerous airs of the Slave Coast. Kings and native slavers brought their slaves to the barracoon, where they were purchased by the factors and kept inside until a ship arrived. The men were secured as a rule, but the women and children were allowed to run loose.

As times changed, the Africans played an even larger role in slaving. One such was the king of Barsally, a very

Tales of the Slave Coast—II

An African slave market

powerful ruler inland. Whenever this king wanted goods or liquor, he would send a messenger to the coast to look for a ship. Finding a slave ship, the king would declare war against some other kingdom, seizing the people as he went, and selling them as slaves. If he was not at war with another kingdom at the time, he would even sack one of his own towns, going in at night with his warriors and setting fire to the grass huts. As the people ran from the flames, they were captured, and their arms were tied behind them. They were marched to the coast and there sold as slaves.

The slave-traders believed that the supply of black slaves was endless, given the temperament of these African kings, who could not stop fighting among themselves. Supply was not the problem, nor in the first half of the nineteenth century was the demand for slaves slackening. The slave-traders' worst problem was a growing sentiment on both sides of the Atlantic among nonslaveholders against the horrors of slavery.

7

Tales of the Middle Passage

Each time an American slave ship set out on a voyage, it made three passages or trips. The first was the passage from the home port to the Slave Coast, with the ship loaded with rum and other trade goods. The second, or "middle passage" was the trip from the Slave Coast of Africa to the New World, with a cargo of slaves. The third passage was the voyage to the home port, when the ship would usually be carrying some other trade goods, usually molasses, which would be made into rum.

But the middle passage had a much more somber meaning, too. When sailors referred to this voyage they were speaking of the long, dangerous trip from east to west across the Atlantic, with a tightly packed load of human cargo that stank and carried disease and death and that sometimes resulted in mutiny and destruction for the captain and crew. The sailors spoke of the middle passage with some awe. It was profitable but dangerous and unpleasant, and for the greater part of the voyage the ship would be passing through the Torrid Zone. From the beginning of the slave trade until the end of it, the conditions on the ships changed very little, except that they were better in the beginning and worse in the end, when the dangers of illegal slave-trading made the captains ready to sacrifice the lives of the slaves on a moment's notice. The Middle Passage, then, was nearly the same in the eighteenth and nineteenth centuries.

The greatest danger to the slave ships always came when they were loading on the African coast. Once aboard the ships, the blacks realized that they were being sent far away from home, and often there was violence before the slave ships sailed. On one slave ship, two strong young men who were shackled together refused to go down the hatch, and when they began to struggle and hurt a crew member, one of them was shot down. He fell across the legs of his companion, but the other fought until he, too, was shot and killed.

What the traders really feared was a general slave uprising, such as one that occurred aboard the ship *Nancy,* out of Liverpool. The *Nancy* was lying off New Calabar with 132 slaves aboard one night when the slaves broke their shackles and freed one another below deck. Then, even though they were unarmed, they swarmed through the hatch and attacked the crew. Blacks ashore came rushing out to the ship, not to help

The slave deck of a ship arriving at Key West, Florida

either slaves or whites, but to plunder the slave ship of her rum and beef during the excitement and to rob the sailors of their possessions. Then the shore party captured the slaves aboard the ship and took them off to sell to other ships, while some blacks fought the sailors to keep them occupied. Finally, the blacks cut the cables and set the *Nancy* adrift, and she ran aground. The captain of another slaver lying in the river sent a boat to rescue the captain and his crew, but the ship was lost.

Other ships were cut off after the captain had once had unfavorable dealings with the native kings. To be cut off meant the captain must move to some other part of the African coast, for he could never again secure slaves in the area where his reputation had gone sour. But mutiny was by far the worst danger (although how a slave can be accused of mutiny is another matter). By 1845 there had been 150 major uprisings, called mutinies, aboard the slavers, some of them ending in the deaths of dozens of slaves, some in the destruction of the ship, as in the case of the *Nancy*.

The case of the *Albion-Frigate* is one that ended badly for the slaves. She was a London slave ship of 300 tons. The crew kept the slave quarters fairly clean while she was in port, washing down the 'tween decks three times a week with pails of vinegar and dropping red-hot bullets into the vinegar to try to erase the stench of a crowded slave ship. As he waited for a full cargo, the captain grew lax. One day the slaves rose up and tried to seize the ship. Some slaves had pieces of iron torn off hatches. Some had broken shackles from their legs and used them as weapons. They attacked and killed one sailor. They so injured the boatswain that he could not move. They cut the cook's throat and wounded three other sailors, one of whom was thrown overboard. But the remainder of the crew rallied, rushed to their guns, and began shooting the slaves down, killing many and wounding others until the uprising was suppressed. Twenty-eight slaves were lost that day, either by shooting or by jumping overboard to escape.

On most slave ships the slaves were fed twice a day, at midmorning and early evening, while in port. The meal was usually a gruel made of beans or peas or wheat, with lard, and sometimes with palm oil or Guinea pepper. After the evening meal the male slaves were taken below decks and put down for the night, but the women and children were allowed more freedom.

On some ships, if the slaves refused to eat, coal or fire was put on a shovel and placed near their lips. Falconbridge said he heard of captains who poured melted lead on slaves who refused to eat. Another device used to make slaves eat was called a *speculum oris*—a mouth opener. It consisted of a pair of dividers with notched ends and a thumbscrew at the blunt end. The legs of the dividers were closed and the ends hammered between the slave's teeth. Then the thumbscrew was worked and the teeth were forced open, so the slave could be force-fed.

Still some slaves refused to eat and starved themselves to death. Other slaves seemed to will themselves to die. Some fell ill from fever and dysentery and passed those diseases along even to the crews of the slave ship. The *Britannia* collected 450 slaves, and lost 230 to smallpox. On the *Elizabeth,* two-thirds of the slave cargo died, and the ship's doctor said they died of "fixed melancholy." One of the most deadly diseases, to crew and slaves alike, was ophthalmia, an eye disease that made men go blind in a few days. Crews and cargoes of slaves were blinded by the swift spread of this disease, and many ships were lost because not one person aboard could see.

The slave ship *Rodeur* set out for Guadeloupe with 162 slaves on board. Ophthalmia set in, and the captain threw thirty-six blacks overboard to save the rest, but within a few days all aboard but one member of the crew had gone blind. Seeing a sail, this man hailed and asked for help, but learned that he had encountered the slave ship, *Leon,* and that *every man* of her crew was also blinded by ophthalmia. The *Rodeur* reached port, the one man saving his sight just that long. The *Leon* was never seen again.

8

The Slave Ships

The early slave-traders used many kinds of ships. Some of the most successful were whaling ships, because they had large, deep holds for carrying whale oil in barrels and capacious decks and great iron pots for the rendering down of blubber. These pots could be used to cook the food for the blacks, and the barrels could carry water or oil.

But soon special ships were built for the slave trade. Most of them had two decks. Between the keel and the lower deck was the area known as the lower hold, which held water, provisions, and goods. The space between the two decks was usually called the 'tween decks. It was the place where the slaves were kept.

One slave ship built in Rhode Island had only three feet, ten inches of 'tween decks—about average for the Newport ships. The deck ran the length and breadth of the ship. A bulkhead or wall was built just behind the main hatch. The men were kept forward, and the women, who were unchained, were allowed aft with the children. The men were forced to lie down with their backs to the deck and their feet extending toward the outsides of the ship. The space allotted to each man was about sixteen inches wide by five or six feet long, and the irons were chained to staples fixed in the deck.

Sometimes slaves were stowed "spoon fashion," which meant lying on their sides, breast to back. Sometimes they were stowed sitting down, each slave crowded into the lap of the man behind him, like riders on a toboggan.

Some captains managed to make a passage humane and livable. They allowed the slaves on deck during the daytime. They fumigated the slave decks with burning tar. They washed the slaves down daily and fed them well, and they let them play their own music. But even captains who were good businessmen lost out in a stormy passage when the hatches had to be battened down and the slaves kept below for days at a time. Under those circumstances all of the slaves might be lost.

The Liverpool slave ships were the worst of all. They had a 'tween decks of a little over five feet, but the captains would not waste space, so on each side a gallery six feet wide was suspended between the two decks, and another row of slaves was laid on that rude planking.

For sanitary facilities the ships usually carried big metal pots, about a foot wide at the top and two feet

The Slave Ships

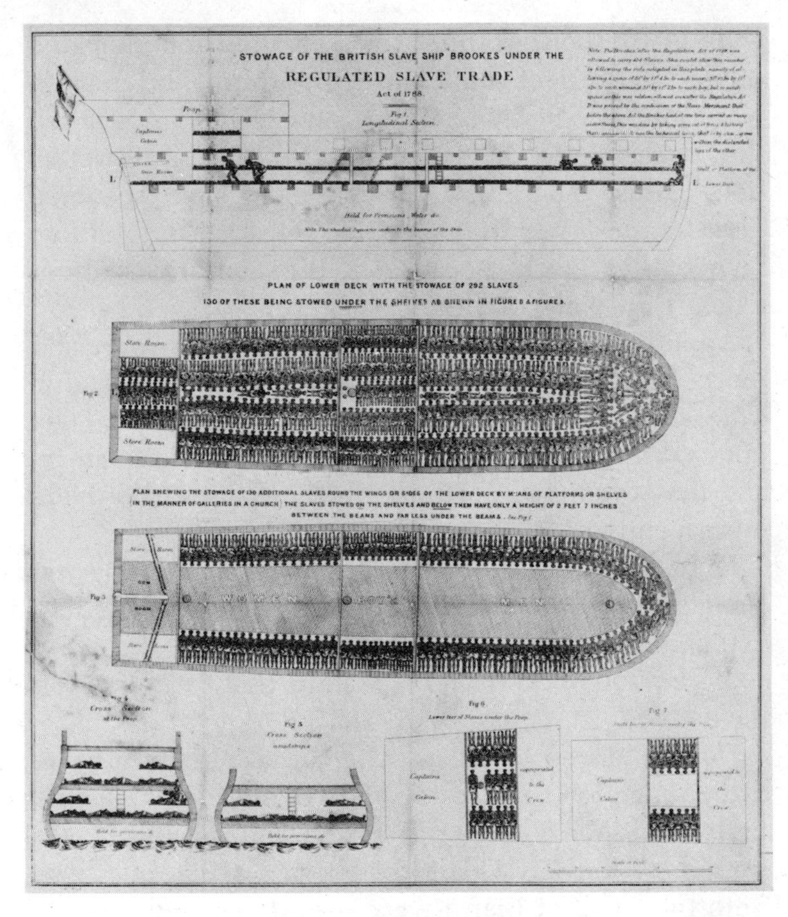

How the slaves were shipped

wide at the bottom. But slaves chained together and stapled to the floor could hardly use them, and the filth was soon indescribable. The crews of the ships hosed the 'tween decks down every morning in self-protection against the stench, but the excrement spawned disease, and it was the rare slave ship that did not lose many of its blacks because of the conditions under which they were carried.

Apparently the Dutch slave-traders were wiser and more humane, and, therefore, the most successful. They did not build racks in their 'tween decks. They built gratings and hatches in the deck to let the air in, and they often had portholes in their ships to provide more ventilation for the slaves.

As to the others—it was said that on a clear day you could smell a French, Portuguese, or English slave ship five miles to leeward, and, unfortunately, the same could be said of the American ships that turned to the slave trade.

Having loaded his slaves, the captain made sure he had enough food and water aboard and that it was the right food. Much of it was purchased locally. Blacks from the Windward Coast liked boiled grains, but those from the Bight of Biafra were used to stewed yams as their principal food. And if the slave-trader did not have the right food, he might have a hunger strike aboard.

At sea the slaves were fed on deck, weather permitting. Alexander Falconbridge served as surgeon aboard several slave ships and later wrote of his experience. This is how the slaves were fed:

> Their food is served up to them in tubs about the size of small water buckets. They are placed around these tubs, in companies of ten to each tub, out of which they feed themselves with wooden spoons. These they soon lose and when they are not allowed others they feed themselves with their hands. In favorable weather they are fed upon deck but in bad weather their food is given them below. Numberless quarrels take place among them during their meals; more especially when they are put upon short allowance; which frequently happens if the passage from the coast of Guinea to the West Indies proves of unusual length. In that case the weak are obliged to be content with a very scanty portion. Their allowance of water is about a half a pint each at every meal.

Some captains were sadists. One of these was Captain Williams, of the brig *Ruby* of Bristol, which slaved off the African coast. If the slaves on his ship would not eat, Captain Williams would have them flogged until they did. He seemed to take pleasure in beating them himself until they bled and in hearing their moans. One slave was flogged repeatedly for two days by the captain and his chief mate until his body was lacerated all over. Then he was given back to the trader on shore, and the trader was forced to provide a new slave.

9

The Horrors Realized

The selling of the slaves in the West Indies and in the Americas was one of the most heinous of occupations. When the ship arrived in the West Indies the slaves were segregated. The sick ones were taken off first and sold, usually at a tavern, either singly, or as a group at public auction. These were purchased by speculators for the most part, for perhaps five or six dollars each. One woman at Panama once bought, for a dollar, a slave who had dysentery. The speculators took the chance that perhaps the slaves would recover, and then they would be worth hundreds of dollars.

In the early days the healthy slaves were usually sold by a method called the scramble. On an appointed day the captains and potential purchasers would meet and determine a fixed price for the slaves aboard the ships, the sick slaves, theoretically at least, having been sold earlier. The blacks were then landed and moved into a large court or yard that belonged to one of the merchants. As soon as the agreed-upon hour arrived, the doors were opened and the purchasers rushed in to claim their slaves. Some would link arms and encircle a group of slaves. Others would carry ropes with which they would claim their prizes. But these slaves were not always as fit as they seemed. One captain had several slaves who were afflicted with flux or diarrhea. He concealed their illness, and the slaves were sold. Sometimes slaves in pain or afflicted with some illness were dosed with drugs so their purchasers would not know their condition. Sometimes slaves who would not eat were force-fed until landing, but would later starve themselves to death.

Captain Luke Collingwood and the *Zong* sailed from St. Thomas Island off the African coast in September, 1781, with a cargo of 440 black slaves and a crew of seventeen men. The flux set in because of overcrowding, before the ship was halfway across the middle passage. Sixty of the slaves died. The dysentery spread to the crew, and seven members of the crew died, too. The ship began to leak badly. Now, aside from the danger of the trip, Captain Collingwood was faced with a vital decision. The condition of the slaves was such that he might not be able to sell most of them in the West Indies. Further, as he announced to the crew, there were only 200 gallons of water left in the casks, which would not carry them all back to safety. The ship's mate, James Kelsal, argued that there was no water shortage. But the captain overruled him. He then selected fifty-four slaves, all of them sick or weak, and threw them overboard. A few days later forty-two more were murdered. A third time, twenty-six slaves were handcuffed together and pushed into the sea, while ten more, chosen to die, preferred to leap to their deaths. Late in December the *Zong* arrived in Jamaica. Captain Collingwood sold the rest of his slaves and sailed back to England.

There the captain and his ship's owners claimed £30 for each of the slaves he had jettisoned, under the admiralty rules that a ship was entitled to compensation from its insurance company if "cargo" had to be jettisoned to save the ship or the crew. The insurance company refused to pay the claim, and the case was taken to court. A court held that slaves were property just like horses, for example, and that the captain had every right to throw the property overboard and claim insurance. The insurance company appealed the case to the Court of the Exchequer, and when the appeal was heard, the judge, Lord Mansfield, said that he had to admit that the law was clearly on the side of the slave-traders. But he also said "a higher law" applied to this shocking case of inhumanity, and he ruled against the captain, because he felt a cargo of slaves should not be treated simply as merchandise.

Such practices and publicity gradually brought to the public attention the horrors of the slave trade. Change was a long time in coming, it seemed, even though forces were at work on both sides of the Atlantic Ocean to try to put an end to the traffic in human flesh.

Some Pennsylvania Quakers were leaders in the

movement in America. They began a campaign in 1693 to put an end to enslavement of the blacks. They had allies in the Puritans of New England, but as long as the trade proved profitable, the Puritans were overruled by the traders of the port cities.

By 1712 the Quakers were working to stop the importation of slaves into the Pennsylvania colony, but since the colony's government was subject to the regulation of the Privy Council in England, nothing came of the attempts to outlaw the trade. Some Quakers joined in a movement to stop using cane sugar, which was raised by slave labor, and used maple sugar, which was made by New England farmers. The leader of this movement was John Woolman, one of the important figures in the Society of Friends.

Another Quaker who was active in the fight against slavery was Anthony Benezet, a son of a French Huguenot family which migrated to the New World. Benezet became a friend of Benjamin Franklin and Benjamin Rush, both of whom were strongly opposed to slavery. Benezet studied the slave trade and wrote several books about this evil, including a report on conditions along the Guinea coast. His books were widely read.

Nor were the Quakers the only opponents of the slave trade. The legislature of Maryland in the eighteenth century passed several laws against slavery and the trade, only to have the laws overturned by the royal governors, who were responsible to the Crown, not to the colonists. Still, no slaves from Guinea were landed in Maryland after 1769.

In other colonies, however, King George III had his

Negroes for Sale.

A Cargo of very fine ſtout Men and Women, in good order and fit for immediate ſervice, juſt imported from the Windward Coaſt of Africa, in the Ship Two Brothers.— *Conditions are one half Caſh or Produce, the other half payable the firſt of January next, giving Bond and Security if required.*

The Sale to be opened at 10 *o'Clock each Day, in* Mr. Bourdeaux's *Yard, at No.* 48, *on the Bay.*

May 19, 1784. JOHN MITCHELL.

Thirty Seaſoned Negroes

To be Sold for Credit, at Private Sale.

AMONGST which is a Carpenter, none of whom are known to be diſhoneſt.

Alſo, to be ſold for Caſh, a regular bred young Negroe Man-Cook, born in this Country, who ſerved ſeveral Years under an exceeding good French Cook abroad, and his Wife a middle aged Waſher-Woman, (both very honeſt) and their two Children. *Likewiſe,* a young Man a Carpenter.

For Terms apply to the Printer.

Announcement of a slave auction

way. The people of Boston petitioned against the landing and sale of slaves in Boston harbor, and so did Salem. But King George warned the colonists that he was most displeased and told the colonial legislatures that they could not pass laws obstructing the sale or importation of slaves in the colonies.

It is not very well known that at the time of the Declaration of Independence there was a good deal of feeling in the colonies against slavery. Many agreed with Thomas Paine, who held that it was ridiculous for the colonists to talk so loudly about "freedom" while they maintained slavery. Patrick Henry owned slaves but admitted that he could not justify the practice morally. So did James Madison. John Adams of Massachusetts refused to own slaves, and so did many other New Englanders.

In the first draft of the Declaration of Independence, Thomas Jefferson, a slaveowner, blamed George III for bringing slaves to the North American continent.

The matter continued to plague Americans. At the end of the revolution, John Jay told the British that the United States intended to abolish the importation of slaves. Some of the states did.

When the confederation of new states was established, many of the statesmen hoped to abolish slavery. Washington and Jefferson both wanted to see the abolition of slavery, and, indeed, both presidents provided in their wills that all their own slaves would be freed on their deaths. Most of the leaders of the American colonies held similar views: Benjamin Franklin, Patrick Henry, James Madison, and Alexander Hamilton all spoke out against slavery. Indeed, in the First Continental Congress, when it came time to set up a system of government for the Northwest Territory, some members of Congress drafted a provision that after 1800 slavery should be illegal in that territory. This was an indication of the thinking of the majority of Americans on the question of slavery. But the vested slave interests of the South arose indignantly—and at the moment it seemed more important to fight the war of independence than to stand on this particular principle.

At the Constitutional Convention in Philadelphia in 1787, the majority of delegates wanted to eliminate slavery from the nation they were establishing, but South Carolina and Georgia rose up in fury and threatened to walk out if this were done. Again, in what was seen as the greater interest of national unity, the majority gave in to the minority on the question of basic human freedom.

The slaveholding southerners wanted specific guarantees in the Constitution for slavery, but the majority were very much opposed. That is why slavery is discussed in idea but not in *words.* For example, in Section 2 of Article I, dealing with representation and taxes, the Founding Fathers referred to "free persons" and to "those bound to service for a term of years" to "Indians not taxed" and to "all other persons." The last were the slaves, and it was so distasteful for the majority to discuss slavery in the Constitution without abolishing it that they resorted to this euphemism.

Again in Section 9 of the same article, the fathers of the nation backed into the issue. The intent of this section was to outlaw slavery. Here is how it was stated: "The Migration or Importation of such Persons as any of the states now existing shall think proper to admit, shall not be prohibited by the Congress prior to the Year One Thousand eight hundred and eight, but a tax or duty may be imposed on such Importation, not exceeding ten dollars for each Person."

Again, the distaste of the Constitutional Convention for slavery was felt, but the power of the southern states to destroy the union before it was even formed was such that the statesmen tried to compromise away their differences and, publicly, in their document, to conceal that terrible word "slavery." It would be seventy-eight years, after the end of a terrible, bloody war, before the word "slavery" would appear in the Constitution, in the Thirteenth Amendment, which abolished the institution of slavery. In 1787, as the Founding Fathers considered the future, they yielded to a South that would not join the confederation if there was tampering with slavery. As Roger Sherman, a signer of the Constitution, put it: "It is better to let the Southern States import slaves than to part with those states."

When the Constitution was accepted and the states planned a union, there was again agitation against slavery and the slave trade. Again the southerners of Georgia and South Carolina prevented effective laws against slavery or the slave trade. But in 1790 Congress resolved that it had the power to legislate in the matter of the slave trade, although not in the matter of slavery. Mild legislation was passed to prohibit the carrying on of the slave trade *from* the United States *to* any other place, but that did not meet the point at all. There was very little trade in slaves *from* the United States; almost all of it was *to* the United States. Congress did say that it could legislate against the slave trade, but not earlier than the year 1808. And that is more or less how matters stood, although the Abolitionists were strong and unflagging in their attempts to secure laws that would put a stop to slavery and the trade.

10

Outlawing the Slave Trade

Early in the eighteenth century some wealthy English families who had moved to the West Indies went home to England once again. They took black slaves with them, having grown accustomed to the service of slavery. When these slaves saw that white servants were free, many of them ran away from their owners. Some learned that under the English law a man baptized in the Church of England was automatically free and so rushed to be baptized.

Such a law existed, but George III and his administrators cared little for the law. The Crown's attorneys wrote an opinion saying that even if a slave was baptized, he remained a slave, and so slavery was countenanced in England.

In 1765, a famous case began, involving the morality of slavery. A planter named David Lisle came to London from the West Indies bringing slaves. Among them was a slave named Jonathan Strong. Lisle lived in Wapping for a time and was so cruel to Strong that the slave collapsed from his beatings. Lisle then threw him into the street to die.

In Wapping at that time lived a doctor named William Sharp who was known widely for his kindness and charity. He discovered Jonathan Strong, treated and cared for him, and the slave recovered. But was he still a slave, having been abandoned by his master?

Dr. Sharp thought not. He sent Jonathan Strong to his brother Granville, who found a job for him. Two years went by, and Lisle learned of Jonathan Strong's whereabouts. He kidnapped him and sold him to a man named John Kerr for £30.

Jonathan Strong tried to escape and was thrown into prison. He got word to Granville Sharp, who went to the lord mayor of London. The lord mayor heard the case and discharged Strong because he had been kidnapped.

Granville Sharp was involved in another legal case related to slavery and the slave trade. A Virginia planter named Charles Stewart had brought a slave named James Somerset to England. Taken by the idea of freedom, Somerset ran away, but was captured and sent to Jamaica to be sold.

Granville Sharp heard of the case and secured a writ of *habeas corpus,* which prevented the transfer. The issue was whether an African slave brought to England became free by stepping on English soil.

The case was tried, and Somerset was freed. Thereafter, any slave-trader was afraid to bring his cargoes into English waters, and the first serious blow to the slave trade had been struck.

Thirteen years later a Cambridge student named Thomas Clarkson won a prize by writing an essay on the subject of the legitimacy of slavery. In his studies he consulted the work of Anthony Benezet and became so immersed in the problem that he decided to devote all his time to the abolition of the slave trade.

He founded the Society for the Abolition of the Slave Trade and became England's leading Abolitionist. He visited the slave ports and made a collection of the instruments of torture, such as the leg shackles and thumbscrews that were used on the slaves. He was nearly murdered in Liverpool by a gang of slave ship sailors. But still he went on talking, listening, and collecting information.

Another figure in the antislavery movement was a member of Parliament named William Wilberforce, who took Clarkson's information and used it in political speeches. Soon West Indian planters raised a fund of £10,000 to fight Wilberforce's antislavery legislation in the House of Commons. Attempts were made to murder both Wilberforce and Clarkson. The slave captains and the owners of the slave ships made ridiculous claims to the British authorities. They talked of the "happiness" of the blacks in the middle passage and told how they were well fed and well treated at all times. When Wilberforce put a bill through the House of Commons, it died in the House of Lords. The forces of slavery were still strong.

In 1805, however, the tide changed. The importation of Africans to any new British colonies was forbidden. British subjects were forbidden to send slaves into *any* other lands. Then a bill was passed in Parliament which prohibited any British vessel from carrying slaves from a British port after May, 1807, and forbade the landing of any slaves in the colonies after March 1, 1808. In other words, the slave trade was outlawed by Britain. So great a victory was this that Wilberforce received the longest and noisiest ovation heard up to that time in the British Parliament.

In America, meanwhile, the slave-trade issue was debated, and some of the support for the trade came from New England. A representative of Rhode Island asked in Congress why the British should be enjoying all the slave trade, while Americans were discouraged from it. A Connecticut representative sneered at attempts to suppress this lucrative trade, as though the Abolitionists were wild-eyed radicals.

Still, public feeling was moving the other way. Congress made it illegal to outfit ships for the slave trade. No American could legally have an interest in a slave ship's voyage. American slave ships were to be captured, and the guilty captains, crews, and owners would be imprisoned for two years and fined as much as $2,000. The slaves were to be forfeited and returned to Africa where they were to be freed.

Yet slave ships continued to call at American ports in states where slavery was not outlawed, particularly at Charleston, South Carolina. This brisk trade infuriated many other Americans. In 1806 Congress began to move to outlaw the slave trade. In his annual message to Congress that year, President Thomas Jefferson advocated such a law, and the next day the necessary legislation was introduced. On March 2, 1807, President Jefferson signed the bill abolishing the trade in the United States, effective January 1, 1808.

But the slaves were old hands at evasion. It made no difference to them what laws the states had passed earlier. They had broken the laws and had brought in black cargoes. One Congressman claimed that in South Carolina, even when slave importation was outlawed, the trade was scarcely slowed down.

For years there had been a brisk slave trade running between Havana and Pensacola, Florida. Approximately one slaver a week came in there.

Pirates and slavers worked the Louisiana coast, and after the War of 1812 a slaver named Louis Aury smuggled slaves successfully into New Orleans and Florida. Smuggling was a very profitable business, earning the smugglers between $250 and $500 for each slave. Aury set up an "admiralty" on Galveston Island, with a commission from the Mexican government. Theoretically, he was prosecuting the naval war of Mexico against Spain, but actually he was little better than a pirate, and his specialty was slave ships. He smuggled thousands of slaves into the United States from this island and later moved his headquarters to Matagordo and to Amelia Island, Florida, which then became the slave-smuggling capital of America.

So much money was to be made in this trade that it

attracted men from everywhere. David Mitchell, the governor of Georgia, quit office in order to become United States senator and agent for the Creek Indians. The Creek lands lay in the wilderness between the Georgia settlements and the lands of Louisiana, where slaves were needed to work the new and growing plantations. Mitchell supervised the shipment of smuggled slaves through the wilderness into the Creek territory and beyond. He was caught in the act and lost his post and his reputation.

World opinion against slavery is further reflected in the actions of other countries. Denmark abolished the slave trade in her possessions (including those in the Caribbean) in 1802. Sweden outlawed the slave trade in 1813, and the Netherlands stopped its participation in 1814. By treaty the British persuaded the Spanish and Portuguese to abolish the trade north of the equator, which was supposed to put an end to the trade in Cuba and the West Indies as well as in North America. France, too, made slave-trading illegal in 1818.

The English slave trade had been abolished as of May 1, 1807, but just before the law was passed, the 300-ton slave ship *Kitty's Amelia* was cleared by the port authorities for a legal slaving voyage. *Kitty's Amelia* carried eighteen guns, and her tough, experienced captain was Hugh Crow, who had been in the Guinea trade for sixteen years. Captain Crow was one of the canniest of the traders, and he kept his death rate down to about 2 percent on most voyages.

The clearing was a technicality. The ship was not

Africans trading their captives of war as slaves

ready in May, and she did not actually sail from Liverpool until July 27, but she was still operating legally. She took on a crew of some sixty men, although on her way down St. George's Channel she lost four sailors, impressed by a British warship that needed to make up its own crew of men.

After seven weeks, *Kitty's Amelia* arrived at Bonny, and there King Holiday came aboard. The king was immensely upset, Captain Crow noted, for he had heard that *Kitty's Amelia* would be the last ship to come to Bonny for slaves.

On this last legal voyage Crow found a dozen ships at Bonny waiting for slaves, and he had to take his turn. During the waiting, fever and dysentery broke out among the crew, and some trade goods rotted and had to be thrown overboard. The sickness delayed the slaving; then storms came up, and the ship dragged her anchors.

In time Captain Crow got his cargo—"as fine a cargo of blacks as ever had been taken from Africa"—but disease struck again. He had two doctors aboard, and they were busy all the time, with blacks and whites dying at such an alarming rate that Crow put into St. Thomas in the Gulf of Guinea to rest and recruit. Those who were in charge of supplies bought dried shrimps from the natives at St. Thomas and made broth for the slaves. They mixed it with flour and palm oil and seasoned it with pepper and salt. They fed the blacks yams and shelled beans and rice together. They mixed soup with peeled yams and pounded biscuit. The sick received meat broth made from mutton and goat and even chicken. In time the sickness seemed to die out, and Crow sailed again. But illness struck another time, and his chief mate died.

Later in the voyage a fire threatened the ship. The fire was put out, and Captain Crow made doubly sure that his slaves were well treated on this voyage, because he had to recoup. It would be his last chance.

Each morning the slaves were brought on deck at about eight o'clock and given water to wash their hands and faces and lime juice to clean their mouths, along with chew-sticks of lime wood for their teeth, and towels to dry with. They were given brandy bitters. At eleven they washed their bodies with palm oil. Each day the men were given pipes and tobacco (the women were given beads), and then they were allowed freedom of the decks. At noon they were fed bread and coconuts. At three o'clock they were given another meal and then sent below at about five o'clock, their slave deck having been scrubbed.

The passage took eight weeks to Kingston, Jamaica. The two doctors died. So did fifty slaves and thirty sailors. But Crow found that there were sixteen other slave ships in the harbor, all in worse shape than his own ship, because they had not taken so much care on the voyage. In these last days everyone was rushing to make as much money as possible. And so Crow prospered and retired from the trade—wearing the debatable honor of being the last legal British slave-trader.

11

Suppressing the Slave Trade

In 1808 slaves were being exported in greater numbers from every creek and beach along the Slave Coast of Africa. Britain imposed a fine of £100 for every slave found aboard a vessel and even went so far as to order that a slaving vessel be confiscated. But the trade persisted, until in 1811 Parliament strengthened the law and made slave-trading an offense punishable by banishment for fourteen years. Later, trading was made a capital offense, and slavery itself was finally abolished throughout the British Empire.

It must be said for the British that once Parliament had been convinced of the need to end the slave trade, the government moved strongly to do so. This was not easy, however.

As they laid their plans for suppression of the slave trade, the British took a good long look at the African coast. There were no formal boundaries of states and governments. But there were some settlements. On Cape Verde stood the town of Goree, near where the modern city of Dakar was built. Then came an area dominated by the Portuguese on the Rio Grande. On the bulge known as the Windward Coast, because of the way the prevailing winds blew, lay Sierra Leone, founded by British Abolitionists in the eighteenth century, with its capital at Freetown. This was to be the major British base for suppression of the African slave trade. A prize court to adjudicate the fate of slave ships was established here, and British naval vessels called at this port regularly.

In the beginning it looked easy. But in spite of the general good will that seemed to exist, no nation took kindly to the British proposal that British ships stop suspected vessels of other nations and search them. A British warship had captured the French slave ship *Louis,* but when the matter came before the court at Sierra Leone, the court gave ship and slaves back to its owner because France had not granted Britain the right to search. Britain then made treaties with other countries to stop the trade. Agreements came and agreements went, and all this time the British attempted to suppress the slave trade across the Atlantic.

One of the greatest problems for the British was the recalcitrance of the Americans. The reluctance of the average American owner to submit to the stopping and searching of vessels stemmed back to the days of the impressment of seamen. But the clever slave-traders played on this reluctance constantly, and so did many

Capture of a large slave ship by the Africa Squadron

politicians and businessmen of the South. Consequently, long after the War of 1812, any British captain who dared to stop an American vessel, slave ship or not, was in trouble. Several times war threatened, for Americans suspected that the British were trying to use the slave trade as a means of suppressing all American trade with other nations.

In 1817 a Court of Mixed Commission was established at Freetown. This was a court representing the various nations that had agreed to abolish slavery or the trade in whole or in part, and when various slave vessels were brought into port, the court adjudicated the cases. Sierra Leone became a colony of free blacks, consisting for the most part of those who had been enslaved and then freed by the British Navy. Later the Americans would establish Liberia, and the French would establish Libreville.

But in the beginning there was only Sierra Leone, and a determined British Navy, whose efforts at slave-trade suppression were divided among three African stations: the northern division; the Bight division, which covered the inner curve of the coast; and the southern division.

At first the British tried to police this long piece of territory with only two vessels, the frigate *Solebay* and the sloop *Derwent.* Obviously it was impossible, as the captains reported by 1809. The next year the Africa Squadron, as it was called, was augmented by four more vessels. These ships began to cause trouble among the slave-traders. It is impossible to escape the realization that at least part of the complaint Americans had against Britain's arrogance in stopping American ships at sea in the early years of the nineteenth century stemmed from the British stopping of American slave ships that were running the slave blockade.

One serious difficulty that the British had not anticipated, when their humanitarianism caused them to suppress the trade, was the growth of the economies of Cuba and Brazil. Suddenly, early in the nineteenth century, a great demand for slaves arose in these countries. And in Europe and the Americas there were hundreds of adventurers who were willing to brave the dangers of sea, sickness, and possible capture in order to acquire a fortune.

Since the traffic was illegal in America, it was impossible to tell precisely how many slaves were moved to the southern states, but the estimates ranged from 10,000 to 20,000 a year.

Also since the slave trade was generally outlawed, it was difficult to secure accurate figures about costs. But in 1854 a slave-trader named Theodore Canot wrote *Adventures of an African Slaver,* describing his adventures in the trade and giving a good account of the costs and profits of a slave voyage in the year 1827.

Expenses Out	
Cost of La Fortuna, a 90 ton schooner	$ 3700
Fitting out, sails, carpenter and cooper's bills	2500
Provisions for Crew and slaves	1115
Wages advanced to 18 men before the mast	900

Wages advanced to captain, mates, boatswain, and cook	440
200,000 cigars and 500 doubloons, cargo	10900
Clearance and hush money	200
	19755
Commission at 5 percent	987
Full cost of voyage out	20742

Expenses Home	
Captain's head money at $8 a head	1746
Mates' head money at $4 a head	873
Second mate and Boatswain's head money at $2 each	873
Captain's wages	219.78
First mate's wages	175.76
Second mate and Boatswain's wages	307.12
Cook and Steward's wages	264
Eighteen sailors' wages	1972
	27172.46

Expenses in Havana	
Government Officers at $8 per head	1736
My commission on 217 slaves, expenses off	5565
Consignee's commissions	3873
Extra expenses of all kinds	1200
Total expenses	39980.46

Returns	
Value of vessel at auction	3950
Proceeds of 217 slaves	77469
	81419
Total returns	$81,419
Total Expenses	39,980.46
Net Profit	41,438.54

These figures told a great deal about the middle passage. Canot had shipped 220 slaves, and only three of them died on the voyage. With the outlawing of the trade, slavers packed the slaves in tighter than ever and seldom allowed them on deck, because it would mean serious trouble if the slaves were seen. Every effort had to be made to keep the slave ship looking like something it was not—an innocent trading vessel.

Rum was no longer the basic medium of exchange on the Slave Coast, either. It was too bulky and too hard to get, once the United States had outlawed the trade. On this trip, Canot's men traded in cigars and silver.

The $200 for clearance and hush money to get out of Havana at the beginning of the voyage was a bribe to the port authorities, who did not charge very much for an unladen vessel. The 5 percent commission was paid to the agent who handled the transaction for Canot.

As for the expenses home, Canot was the entrepreneur, and he employed a captain and crew, who received salary and "head money"—at least the officers did—for the slaves they brought back. The head money encouraged captain and officers to be careful of the human cargo.

Expenses in Havana included $8 per head, most of which went to the governor of Cuba, for he received a bribe for every slave who came into the island, the Spanish slave trade having theoretically been outlawed above the equator.

The slave dresses, which cost $2 each, were rude bits of ill-fitting cloth. To keep the slaves as clean as possible, they were shipped across the ocean stark naked.

Not all voyages were so profitable, of course, because on some a far larger number of slaves were lost, and sometimes expenses might run much higher. But with $40,000 to be made on a single voyage, the risk seemed well worth the taking. And so the slave traffic continued despite the British effort to suppress it.

With the outlawing of the trade, its nature changed somewhat, too. The factors on the coast of Africa became very important men, and they enlarged their slave pens, where they might keep hundreds of slaves. One of the changes involved speed of loading. With the Africa Squadron patrolling the coast, a slaver never knew when a British man-of-war might come down on the harbor, and therefore it was important to get in, get loaded, and get out again.

A trader once came to New Sestros on the Ivory Coast and found a large cargo of slaves waiting there. But a British warship was lying in the harbor, blockading the coast. The slaver simply stood offshore and waited. After some time the British warship sailed away to Sierra Leone because her captain had to secure supplies and patrol more areas. Then the slaver sailed in near shore. In twenty-four hours the slave ship loaded 120 slaves, although the heavy wind and surf upset just about every other canoe that was taken through the breakers, forcing the slaves and boatmen to swim for their lives. At the end of twenty-four hours, the mastheads of the British warship showed again on the horizon, and the slaver departed in haste, without all its cargo, but with enough to make a handsome profit.

One might say, from the standpoint of the British Navy, that when His Majesty's government decided to try to wipe out the slave trade, the gentlemen of Parliament did not know how difficult a task they had chosen. Nonetheless, the British Navy tried, and its efforts were gallant, if not always successful.

In 1818, Britain sent Commodore Sir George Collier to the Gulf of Guinea with the H.M.S. *Tartare,* and the H.M.S. *Inconstant.* A year later he had six ships under his command, ranging from the thirty-six-gun H.M.S. *Tartare* to the twelve-gun H.M.S. *Thistle.* For most of the next fifty years the British maintained the squadron.

The Bonny and Calabar rivers became the favorites of the slave-traders. In three months, Lieutenant T. H. Rothery, in the ship H.M.S. *Snapper,* captured twenty-eight slave-traders, twenty of them Portuguese. Still the slave ships came in. And as time went on, and the American government took a strong line against ship stopping, slave-traders began to claim the protection of the American flag.

In the spring of 1821 the H.M.S. *Tartare* captured the 200-ton schooner *Anna Maria* in the bight off the African coast, and the British discovered to their horror that below decks her captain had crammed 500 slaves on a slave deck two feet eleven inches high. When the British boarded, the captain blustered that he was an American, Matthew Smith, and that they would pay for their insolence. But his papers proved that he was Spanish, that his name was Matteo Sanches, and that the ship was Cuban.

In such an affair the British captain always ran a serious risk because of his country's regard for the spirit and letter of the law. For example, Commander Meredith of H.M.S. *Pelorus* stood off the New Calabar River and watched a slave ship load 600 slaves. He moved in to take her. She moved to shore and unloaded. After several loadings and unloadings the British captain made his own men put the slaves aboard the slave ship and then sent her to Sierra Leone for trial. There the Mixed Commission held that the British captain had acted improperly, and he was fined £1,800 for illegal behavior. The court held that the captain had to catch the slave ships with slaves the slave-traders had loaded themselves.

12

Tales of the Africa Squadron

Just about everything, it seemed, worked for the slavers against the Africa Squadron, including its own ships. The British were sailing the slow, dignified ships of Nelson's time. The slavers were building and buying fast topsail schooners and brigs, called "clippers," because of their speed. Finally, however, the Admiralty caught on, and the British Navy began buying up some of these fast Baltimore clippers after they were caught and condemned. One such slaver turned slave-chaser was the *Black Joke,* which had been named the *Henriquetta* until she was captured. This fast ship carried only a single, long, eighteen-pound gun on a pivot. But she became a tender to the flagship of the British Africa Squadron, and a very effective slave-ship catcher. Two years later another fast clipper, the *Fair Rosamond,* was captured and put into service. Between them, these two vessels captured nine slave ships in two years.

One day the *Fair Rosamond* captured the Spanish slaver *La Pantica,* and took her into a prize court for adjudication. A third of her slave cargo was on deck, but two-thirds were kept below. By the time the ship arrived in port, the slaves on deck were nearly dead from heat and disease. Below decks, the slaves were even worse off. The ship stank from stem to stern, and it was learned that on the voyage from Old Calabar, forty-one of the slaves had died.

The slaves were taken off the ship, and after she had been condemned they were offered their choice: they could go to the West Indies as free apprentices; they could join the British forces as soldiers; or they could settle in the Sierra Leone colony on lands provided by the British. In the years between 1818 and 1834, some 30,000 slaves were liberated at Sierra Leone from nearly eighty ships captured. Most remained in Africa.

Slavers sometimes were hauled into other ports, such as Surinam, Rio de Janeiro, and Havana, but Sierra Leone was by far the most used port, because the best place to catch slavers in the wide Atlantic was along the Slave Coast itself. The fast ships had much too great a chance to escape if they made the open sea.

One of the great chases was made by the cruiser *Pickle.* She had been ordered to cruise off the north coast of Cuba in 1829 to intercept slavers bringing cargoes to Havana harbor. One evening the *Pickle* was sailing close in to shore when her captain, Lieutenant J. McHardy, saw a heavily laden vessel approaching her. There was very little wind, but the British crew wet down the sails and trimmed them in tight to take every advantage of the puffs. By nightfall they had fetched up on the stranger and could fire a warning shot. The shot did not bring a display of her colors, as would be the case with most legitimate vessels.

The British prepared for a night fight. Hardly had this preparation for action been taken when the *Pickle* was struck by a broadside and a rain of musket fire from the other ship. The other, the British quickly learned, carried eighteen guns, while they had only an eighteen-pounder on a pivot and two eighteen-pound carronades.

That first broadside struck down three British sailors out of a crew of thirty-nine. As the fighting went on, other men fell, until eight more Britons were down. But at short range the British were able to use their carronades, into which they crammed ball and chain, and heavy ball for use against the rigging. After half an hour the other ship's mainmast fell, and she surrendered. She was found to be a slaver with 350 slaves aboard. The slaver was sent in to Havana to be handed over to the authorities of the Mixed Commission.

In the early years of the Africa Squadron, the captains and crews earned handsome bounties for their work. On one voyage the H.M.S. *Mosquito* laid claim to £4,945 for the capture of three slavers carrying 380 slaves. But as time went on the bounties were reduced to £10 per head, and then to £5 pounds per head. Oddly enough, the bounties were to become instrumental in encouraging the trade, because payment was only for slaves captured. There was no payment for stopping slave-trade vessels from loading. So, in order to collect, the British captains had to let the slavers embark their cargoes. As a result, many slave ships escaped. Still, between 1839 and 1843 the fast ship *Waterwitch* caught enough slavers to earn more than £2,500 for her captain and about half as much for the admiral in charge of the squadron. (The poor able-bodied seamen had only about £180 to be shared among them. But no one has ever said that the nineteenth-century British Navy was kind to its enlisted men.)

Sometimes the efforts of the Africa Squadron backfired, as in the chase by the *Black Joke,* which surprised two slavers, the *Rapido* and the *Regulo,* one night in 1832. The slavers were just moving out of the Bonny River when the British ship came upon them. The slavers began throwing their blacks overboard, manacled in pairs. The race became a contest to see whether the British could catch them before they had stripped the ships of the slaves, for if the slavers were able to destroy the evidence, they could not be taken as prizes. The *Regulo* was caught with more than 200 of her 450 slave cargo still aboard. The *Rapido* had managed to get rid of every man and woman, but two of them were saved by the British from the sharks, and they testified that they had been aboard the ship. So both slavers were taken that day.

Not always did it work so. One night a British cruiser approached the African coast and came upon the brig *Brillante.* The British ship swooped down (along with three others) and found Captain Homans standing on his deck, surrounded by the smell of slaves, and the hot pots which held food that had been obviously cooked for slaves. But there was not a slave aboard the ship. What had happened to them? Later it was learned that Homans had bound his slaves to the anchor chain, which was stretched around the ship. When the British had come upon him, he dropped his anchor, carrying 600 slaves to their deaths. The tale might have been fictitious as some believe, but it could have happened on the Slave Coast, so small was the regard of the slavers for human life.

One of the famous tales of the slaver chases concerned the *Josephine*, the fastest slaver sailing out of Havana in the 1840s. At dawn on April 30, 1841, seventeen days out from the African coast, the *Josephine* was sailing westward at about six degrees south latitude, off Ambriz. She had recently eluded no fewer than three British cruisers which had tried to catch her with a load of slaves, on the way from Whydah to Havana.

Captain E. H. Butterfield, in the *Fantome*, sighted the *Josephine* and gave chase. He ordered his crew to shake out all the ship's sails, and with every stitch of canvas she began to make eleven knots. The slaver did the same and sped on ahead. But by afternoon, Captain Butterfield could see that he was coming up on the *Josephine*. Through his glass he watched as the slave-ship crew cut away her anchors and jettisoned her long gun to lighten the ship. By evening the cruiser was still drawing up, slowly.

That night, as pursuer raced after pursued, a storm began to rise, and at one o'clock in the morning, the bright moonlight was blotted out by a tremendous squall of wind and rain, which caught the *Josephine* and nearly swamped her. Captain Butterfield kept as much sail as he dared, as they sped through the storm, and when they emerged from it, he found himself running level with the slaver.

Early in the morning of May 1, the British cruiser fired a shot across *Josephine*'s bow, and the chase was ended.

One of the most important combinations of captain and ship that appeared in the squadron was that of Captain H. J. Matson and the H.M.S. *Waterwitch.* Matson made his reputation on the Slave Coast beginning in 1825 when he commanded the gun brig H.M.S. *Clinker,* during which time he liberated 1,400 slaves. He then set to chasing pirates for a time, but in the five years between early 1839 and late 1843 he became the terror of the slavers when the *Waterwitch* came under his command.

In the 1830s a number of wealthy British yachtsmen were trying to improve the design of the British naval brig. After several attempts they achieved a prototype, called the *Pantaloon,* and the *Waterwitch* was copied from that design. She was 90 feet long and 29 feet in the beam, with a displacement of 324 tons. She carried nearly 10,000 square feet of sail. Under Matson and his successor she captured forty slavers.

Another important figure in the suppression of the

trade was Captain Joseph Denham. In 1834, in command of the ten-gun H.M.S. *Curlew* off the coast of Brazil, he captured the first slaver taken in South American waters. He took her into Rio de Janeiro, but the court there said he must go to Sierra Leone, and he took naval vessel, slaver, and 500 slaves back to Africa, only to learn that because the slaver was captured below the equator he must let it go its way. The Portuguese vessel, therefore, carried the slaves across the Atlantic for the third time.

In 1839 Captain Denham was appointed to the H.M.S. *Wanderer,* a fast eight-gun schooner. By this time, through his efforts and those of others, the British government had modified its rules about slave capture. No longer did the cruisers have to actually catch the slaves aboard in order to condemn a vessel; it was enough if such as leg irons and handcuffs were found aboard.

With this new authority Captain Denham chose to stand off the Gallinas River, which was the headquarters of the most notorious slaving group in Africa. For many years the Gallinas estuary had been the location of the barracoons of Don Pedro Blanco. Don Pedro built lookout posts 100 feet high on the low coastal plain. He built a palatial residence, offices, and barracoons. Just before the coming of Captain Denham, Don Pedro retired with his fortune to Havana, but other Spaniards and Portuguese took over his interests on the Slave Coast, and the post continued as the leading slave establishment in the area.

Slaves were thrown overboard when the Africa Squadron approached a slave ship

In the summer of 1840 the British ships H.M.S. *Wanderer*, H.M.S. *Rolla*, and H.M.S. *Saracen* moved back and forth outside the river mouth, letting in any ships which chose to go, but letting no ships out without an inspection.

The Havana merchants on the other end of the slave trade did not know that the Gallinas River was under such close watch. Nine slave ships arrived and were bottled up in the estuary, their crews chafing. With so many slaves waiting for shipment, the barracoons became overcrowded, sickness set in, and the slaves began to die. The *Rolla* sent a ship's boat into the estuary and it swamped. The Spaniards ashore did nothing to help the struggling British sailors, but the sailors made their way through the shark-filled waters to safety.

One day Captain Denham received orders from the governor of Sierra Leone to rescue two black British subjects held in slavery by the king of Gallinas, and this order gave him the excuse he wanted. He took his ships close inshore and then landed his men in boats. Island after island in the estuary was occupied by a barracoon, and Denham set guards over them, while the Spaniards fled inland, followed by their native soldiers.

Once the area was securely in British hands, Captain Denham sent a message to the king of Gallinas, demanding the return of British subjects and insisting that the king sign a treaty with England to abolish the slave trade in his land. Faced with Denham's threat of invasion if he did not sign, the king gave up the British citizens and put his mark on the treaty. He agreed to expel the foreign slave-traders and stop the trade and gave Denham explicit permission to burn the barracoons.

So Denham's men set to work. From one barracoon they moved to the next, freeing the slaves and sending them out to the ships, lest they be captured again by the coastal tribes. After 850 slaves had been rescued, the barracoons were then set afire and burned to the ground.

A precedent was set. Soon Captain H. W. Hill took the boats of the *Saracen* and the *Ferret* in and burned the barracoons at the mouth of the Shebar River. A year later Captain Nurse destroyed the barracoons on the Pongos River north of Sierra Leone. Captain Matson destroyed slave-trade posts at Kabenda and Ambriz.

The British government at home quavered for a while, wondering if these actions were strictly legal. Meanwhile the slave-traders had nerve enough to bring suits in English courts against Denham and Matson. But the suits were dismissed, and the suppression of the trade became more effective. It could be said that during the 1840s, as the demand for slaves grew stronger and stronger, the pressure was definitely being exerted by Great Britain in its most effective way.

The feeling of the British officers and men grew stronger, too, when some of their own men were murdered by slavers. The most notable case occurred in 1845, when the Brazilian slave ship *Felicidade* was captured by the H.M.S. *Wasp.* The captain of the British ship assigned a lieutenant and eighteen men as a prize crew, for although this vessel did not have any slaves she was equipped as a slaver, and it was apparent that she was heading for the African coast to pick up a cargo.

The lieutenant's orders were to keep up with the H.M.S. *Wasp.* This was easy enough, for *Felicidade* sailed better than H.M.S. *Wasp* did. Therefore when the two ships sighted another brigantine that was suspect, *Felicidade* quickly outdistanced the awkward warship, and caught the other. She turned out to be the *Echo,* a Brazilian ship, with 400 slaves on board.

The lieutenant now had a real problem. He had to take seven men aboard the *Echo* as a prize crew, leaving only a midshipman and nine others aboard the *Felicidade* to guard the crew of twenty-one men. They waited for the *Wasp*, but she did not come up, and the two prize crews parted company.

On board the *Felicidade* that night the British sentry and two other sailors fell asleep. The midshipman was taking a bath and was unarmed, talking to the quartermaster, when the Brazilian crew rose up, killed all the sleeping men with knives, and then rushed the others. They threw the midshipman and the other members of the prize crew overboard, hoisted their Brazilian colors, and sailed away to the *Echo*. They caught her, threatened the lieutenant, but then sheered off and ran away.

Three days later the six-gun British brig *Star* caught the *Felicidade* and carried out a routine search. The *Star*'s captain, R. J. W. Dunlop, became suspicious when bloodstains were found on deck. The captain of the *Felicidade* and his servants confessed what had happened but said they had had no part in it. The mutineers were seized and put in irons and taken home in the *Star* for trial.

A lieutenant of the *Star* and a prize crew were put aboard the *Felicidade* to take her to St. Helena, where a prize court had been established. But the *Felicidade* was destroyed in a storm, and the men drifted on a small raft for twenty days until rescued by the brig *Cygnet*. The captain of the slaver and two of his men died from drinking salt water.

The mutineers were taken to England where most of

them were found guilty of murder. The case was appealed, and eventually the slavers were all freed because Britain did not have a treaty with Brazil that covered capture of a slave ship without slaves. This strange turn of justice aroused strong feelings in Britain against all slavers and especially spurred on the British Navy to track down and stop the masters of the slave trade.

13

America's Africa Squadron

One of the first American efforts under the law of 1808 against importation of slaves was carried out by the U.S. Navy in 1811. In January of that year, Secretary of the Navy Paul Hamilton wrote the commander of the Charleston naval station that many slave ships were calling at St. Mary's, Georgia, and asked him to send gunboats there to suppress the trade. In 1814, Navy Commodore D. T. Patterson and Army Colonel George T. Ross were sent to destroy a piratical slave station established by Pirate Jean Lafitte at Barataria Bay, south of New Orleans. The market at Barataria was famous then for selling blacks at a dollar a pound, and the size of the operation is indicated by the fact that the ships and property captured at Barataria were valued at $50,000, at a time when a good vessel could be bought for $3,000.

In 1818, when General Andrew Jackson seized Pensacola from the Spanish, his forces captured the slaver

Constitution which had eighty-four slaves aboard, and the *Louisa* and the *Marino,* which had twenty-three slaves between them. The next year, under President Monroe's urging, Congress strengthened the anti-slave-trade laws of the United States. This came about for several reasons. One was the purchase of Florida in 1819. This put the American government flatly up against the problem. Until this time the brisk trade had been conducted from Havana to Spanish Florida, south of the Perdido River, and even in 1818 the slave trade had been carried on openly and profitably there. By 1817 Portugal and Spain had outlawed the trade north of the equator, but the United States still refused to sign a treaty with Britain, giving the British Navy the right to search ships flying the American flag, no matter what their purpose. In 1818 George Canning, the British foreign secretary, suggested again that the United States cooperate. Secretary of State John Quincy Adams refused to consider this, so Canning made the countersuggestion that the United States send American ships out to do the work. Ship captains were known to carry two or three sets of papers with them, almost always including an American set. Then, if a British man-of-war came up on a slaver, she would run up the American flag, and the British would be powerless to search her. Or the ship might be "sold" to an American sailor aboard, to give her the protection of the flag. Some slavers carried an American supercargo, whose sole function was to take charge of the ship, in his own name, if it was stopped by a British warship.

Canning's suggestion was so reasonable that Monroe and Adams, who were both opposed to the slave trade, took steps to strengthen the laws and cooperate with the British. The new law of 1819 carried an appropriation of $100,000 to support it.

In 1820 three American ships were dispatched to the Slave Coast of Africa: the twenty-gun *Cyane,* under Captain Edward Trenchard; the eighteen-gun corvette *Hornet,* under Captin George C. Reed; and the twenty-four gun corvette *John Adams,* under Captain H. S. Wadsworth. They sailed to the accompaniment of jeers and complaints from the American press and public. No one believed the talk about American ships taking part in attacking the slave trade.

Then came the shock. The *Cyane* sailed in January. On April 10, at the mouth of the Gallinas River, her lookouts sighted seven ships which immediately hoisted their sails and stood out to sea. There was a good offshore breeze that day, and the chase was vigorous for an hour. But then the wind dropped, and Captain Trenchard sent his boats out to the slavers. One was the schooner *Endymion,* whose captain tried to escape in a boat. He was overtaken and turned out to be Alexander McKim, a former U.S. Navy midshipman. There was no doubt about *his* being an American.

Not long afterward, the *Hornet* took an American slaver. Then the schooner *Alligator,* under Captain R. F. Stockton, reached the Slave Coast on May 6 and two weeks later captured four slave schooners at Tradetown near Cape Mesurado. These were American-built ships, and the captains knew it. Trenchard had said earlier that as far as he could see, all the slavers on the coast in 1820 were American-built. But when the ships were taken back to New York, the Spanish government protested that they had Spanish papers, and the French government also protested. If the Americans would not allow the British to stop and search American vessels, what right did the Americans have to interfere with others?

Secretary of State John Quincy Adams in 1820 had no ready answer to the argument, so the ships were released, and the navy was ordered to take only bona fide American slavers in the future. Naturally, when the word got out, the bona fide American slaver practically disappeared from the coast, unless a British vessel was trying to do the boarding.

The *Cyane* soon reported that there were 300 slavers on the Slave Coast. She had captured ten American slavers, but all of them were so thoroughly covered by Spanish papers that she could not act.

The American naval schooner *Shark* came to African waters under Captain Matthew C. Perry, who saw no sign of American slaving at all, although slavers sailed all around him. But that was not unusual then or later, among American officers. Other naval officers sent out to suppress the slave trade were members of southern slaveholding families.

Secretary of State Adams made a further effort to stamp out the slave trade during the last year or so of the Monroe administration. He consented to a treaty which would outlaw the slave trade as piracy, with each nation to try its own nationals, but with anyone able to seize a suspected slave-trader. The United States Senate crippled the measure, and it died.

By 1825 the issue of slavery was becoming so important a domestic problem in the United States that no sensible measure could have passed. The British kept trying to secure American cooperation, but a succession of slaveholding presidents (Jackson, Polk, Taylor, for example) would not be expected to show much enthusiasm, and slaveholding congressmen kept Congress from acting.

For nearly fifteen years, then, the slave trade prospered as never before. The Africa Squadron of the United States Navy was small and was kept small and ineffectual. Slavers plied boldly back and forth across the Atlantic. If a British man-of-war came along, the slaver flew the American flag. If an American man-of-war came along—which was most infrequent—the ship hoisted a Spanish flag.

The trade increased, even doubled, over the days when slave-trading was legal. If American officers went out with the highest ideals, they were soon disabused, as was Lieutenant John S. Paine, captain of the schooner *Grampus.* Paine was sent to Africa with the task of suppressing the slave trade, and he believed his orders. Soon, however, he discovered the truth—that ships he knew to be American had two sets of papers. They showed him their foreign papers, so he could do nothing. The British suggested that he stop a ship that

Capture of a slaver off the coast of Cuba

had non-American papers and hold her until a British warship could come up. He and Commander William Tucker of the British Navy agreed to this plan, but when Paine reported the plan to Washington he was informed coldly that it was against American policy and was then ordered to suppress American slave-traders along the 1,500 mile coast of Africa *with his one ship.*

In the 1830s and early 1840s British-American relations were far from good. The two nations squabbled incessantly over half a dozen matters. The northeast and middle western American-Canadian boundaries were in question. There had been a problem of American-Canadian relations during a Canadian rebellion, which led to the burning of the ship *Carolina* and much ill-feeling. And there was the constant, exasperating matter of the slave trade.

In 1842 Secretary of State Daniel Webster met with the special British Minister Alexander Baring, Lord Ashburton, and worked out a satisfactory treaty which settled these other matters and provided for the American maintenance of an adequate fleet on the African coast to make some dent in the slave trade. The United States was to maintain a squadron with a strength of at least eighty guns. The British had almost twice as many.

The intent of the Webster-Ashburton treaty was to push a large number of American vessels into the suppression of the trade. But that is not quite how it worked out. In 1843 the British had fourteen vessels with a total of 141 guns assigned to slave-trade suppression. The Americans had two ships with thirty guns.

Even the next year, the Americans had only four ships out. The ships were large, in order to carry all the guns, and not at all suited to the task that faced them. Furthermore, the ships were never all on the coast at the same time.

Captain Matthew Perry, serving as a commodore because he had more than one ship, was sent to work out of Monrovia, Liberia, to help enforce the law. He had no enthusiasm for the task, even if he had possessed the proper ships. The way to catch slavers under these conditions was through joint cruising. If a British and an American ship cruised together, it would not make any difference what flag the slaver hoisted, since one or the other would be able to take her. But there was no joint cruising as long as Perry was in command of the squadron. To be fair to Commodore Perry, it must be said that the temper of the times was against ardent suppression, and his instructions were not so much aimed at suppressing the trade as at preventing outright abuse of the American flag at sea.

Lieutenant Commander Andrew Hull Foote was the most effective American officer of the Africa Squadron. He went out to the African coast as commander of the brig *Perry* and tried to do his job well, cooperating fully with the British Squadron. But how much could he do, and how effective could his cooperation be? The captain of the first American slaver Foote captured admitted cheerfully that he had been taken because of his own stupidity. He had a number of sets of papers and flags aboard, he said, and had he not believed the *Perry* was an English ship, he would never have put up the American flag. He also said he had fended off the British time and again by use of that American flag.

There was the real problem—the American sensitivity to "search and seizure" which kept Foote spending much of his time making sure that the British were not interfering with legitimate American vessels (as if there were many of those in the African trade).

From time to time the captains did catch a prize. One such was the *Pons*. Her captain had brought the bark *Pons* from the United States in 1845 and in November of that year she lay off the shore at Kabenda loading slaves. For three weeks the British cruiser *Cygnet* stood offshore, and the *Pons* did not move. Then, on November 30, the *Cygnet* had to return to Sierra Leone for water and supplies. That night the *Pons* moved out along the coast, with 903 slaves under her deck. The coast seemed to be clear of all cruisers, British and American.

The next morning the captain of the *Pons* saw a cruiser ahead. He ordered the American flag hoisted, which would be adequate protection against British search and seizure. As it turned out, however, the cruiser was an American, and the hoisting of the American flag gave just the excuse needed to stop the ship and discover the slaves, who were loaded deep in the hold atop the water casks, without even a slave deck to carry them. So bad were their accommodations that eighteen had died in the one night they had been aboard.

The American naval officers saw another example of the slavers' tricks. An American captain was in charge of the vessel, but he also had a Portuguese captain and Portuguese papers aboard. If he saw an American ship coming, he normally would have turned the ship over to the Portuguese.

The voyage of the *Pons* to Liberia was a singularly unhappy one. One hundred and fifty more slaves died on the way because they were so tightly jammed in, and another eight died in the harbor before they could be unloaded.

One reason for the increasing American vigilance might have been the growing arrogance of the slavers. Earlier, the slavers had been circumspect, but at the end of the War of 1812, a number of privateersmen who had taken to the adventurous life went into a trade of their own. Five famous ships were the *Commodore Perry,* the *Commodore McDonough,* the *Argus,* the *Criterion,* and the *Saucy Jack.* They went to Africa, equipped with several sets of papers, and traded for slaves or kidnapped the natives, whichever seemed more profitable. If they came across a slaver smaller than themselves, they hijacked the cargo. If they saw a British or American warship, they ran or fought. In time all but the *Saucy Jack* were captured.

The Brazilian slaver *Velos Passegero* carried twenty guns and a crew of 150 men. With 555 slaves aboard, she fell in with the smaller British H.M.S. *Primrose* (a sloop) and decided to fight. Forty-six of her crew were killed and twenty wounded before she surrendered.

The *Pons* and other slavers were much more businesslike about their affairs. By 1845, for example, when the United States brig *Truxton* captured the schooner *Spitfire* in the Rio Pongo, that 100-ton ship was carrying 346 slaves between decks. The 'tween decks was so low that the men could not sit upright. The slaves were given half a pint of rice and a pint of water a day. The attitude had changed: no longer was it good business to treat slaves well. The theory was to jam them in, rush them across the Atlantic, and accept some losses as a part of the trade.

America's Africa Squadron did continue to make some important captures. One was made in 1850, by Captain Foote, who arrived off Ambriz in the *Perry* on June 5, looking for the American ship *John Adams*, but found she had gone off to Loanda. The next day Foote saw a big ship heading in toward the coast. She had two tiers of painted ports. When the *Perry* came up, the strange ship hoisted her flag—the Stars and Stripes—and on her stern could be seen her name, the *Martha*, of New York. The *Perry* still did not fly her flag, but sent a boatload of boarders to take a look at the ship. As they came around under her stern, the men aboard the *Martha* recognized the American uniforms, and the American flag was quickly hauled down and replaced by a Brazilian flag.

Lieutenant Rush, the boarding officer, went aboard the *Martha* and was met by a Portuguese who claimed to be the captain. Where were her papers? She had none, he said. All right, said Lieutenant Rush, then she must be a pirate.

While this exchange was going on, word came from

the *Perry* that something had been thrown overboard on the far side of the *Martha* as the boat came up on the starboard. The boat crew went around to port and found a writing desk floating in the water. The desk was picked up and opened, and the papers were found, identifying the ship as American. Her real captain was found—an American who had concealed himself as a member of the crew.

There was no doubt about the ship's purpose. Below decks the boarders found supplies of farina and beans, 400 wooden spoons, iron bars, chains, leg irons, and other instruments that could be useful only in the slave trade. The captain had expected to ship 1,800 slaves aboard this vessel in one night and to have cleared the coast the next day.

The *Martha* was taken to New York and condemned. The captain was released on $3,000 bail, but he jumped bail and escaped. The mate was tried and sent to prison for two years.

The slave trade continued right up until the Civil War, and in 1860 it was very brisk indeed. One of the most successful slave vessels was the clipper ship *Nightingale.* She had been built for the California trade, but when that began to slacken off with the increase of steamers on the run, she was converted to a slave ship. In April, 1860, the captain of the U.S.S. *Sumter* wrote home from Africa that the *Nightingale* had shipped a cargo of 2,000 blacks. She was known as a slaver, but she still had not been caught.

In January, 1861, the *Nightingale* was reported at St.

Thomas, off the African coast, but she dodged the authorities. In April she was anchored at Kabenda. The captain of the sloop-of-war *Saratoga* recognized her and went aboard her. He saw nothing out of the ordinary, but got the distinct impression that the ship was making ready to pick up a slave cargo. So the captain went back to his ship and moved away. He came back that very night, anchored not far off, and, in the dark, sent two boats to approach the big clipper ship. The men in the boats surprised the crew of the other ship and boarded her. They found 961 slaves aboard.

The *Nightingale* was taken to Liberia where the slaves were freed, but 160 of them had been abused so badly that they died on the way there. After the slaves were unloaded in Liberia, the ship was then sent to New York under a prize crew and sold. The captain was sent with his ship, but he escaped on the way back to New York when the ship stopped for water at St. Thomas. It was not unusual for American slave ship captains to "escape" even when American naval prize crews were aboard their ships. A good many of the officers of the American Africa Squadron were southerners, and when it came to delivering slave-ship captains to the authorities for trial, they sometimes grew very nearsighted when the ships were unguarded and in port.

14

The *Amistad* Affair

At the height of the American slave trade, several incidents occurred which persuaded people of goodwill in the nonslave states that the whole concept of human slavery was destructive to the nation and to individuals involved in it. One such incident was the *Amistad* Affair, so called because it concerned the slave ship *L'Amistad.*

The *Amistad* Affair began on the coast of Africa in the spring of 1839. A Portuguese slave ship, the *Tecora,* called at the Gallinas River on the Slave Coast and picked up a cargo of "mixed slaves"—men, women, and children—at the infamous barracoon there. When the slaves were loaded, the *Tecora* sailed for Havana, where she arrived safely on June 12.

Theoretically, the importation of slaves into Havana had ended in 1820, when the Spanish government signed an agreement with the British—the general agreement outlawing the slave trade above the equator. Actually, slaves came in by the thousands, most of them for transshipment to the islands of the Caribbean or to the United States. The *Tecora*'s slaves were brought on deck on the night of June 11 when the ship was a few miles off shore. They were loaded into small boats and landed a few miles below Havana. From there, roped together, they were walked to a barracoon owned by a slave-dealer in Havana.

Men began to visit the barracoon to buy slaves. Among the visitors were José Ruiz and Pedro Montez. Ruiz claimed to be a planter with land on the Isle of Pines. He was a handsome figure, dressed in tropical whites with lace at his throat and his cuffs. Smoking slim black cigars, he negotiated with the slave-dealers, inspected the slaves carefully, and bought forty-nine of them. He said he was taking them to his estate. (Later, others were to say he was a middleman for the transshipment of slaves from Cuba to the southern American states.) Montez, a retired sea captain, bought three little girls, the oldest twelve years old, and said he would take them to his home in the Cuban province of Puerto Príncipe as personal servants.

The two men conferred and agreed to ship their slaves together aboard the schooner *L'Amistad*, which was owned and operated by Captain Ramon Ferrar. *L'Amistad* was a fast schooner of the type often used in the slave trade. She had been built in Baltimore and was a sound ship, about 120 tons, with a black hull and strong new canvas. Captain Ferrar, no matter what he had done with her in the past, was now in the interisland coasting trade, and he earned his living by carrying mixed cargoes from one end of Cuba to the other, or perhaps to the British West Indies. If he ever took human cargoes into the southern American ports, he certainly did not admit it, for it was legal to move slaves about Cuba, where slavery was still legal, though foreign trade in slaves was not. When Captain Ferrar agreed to accept the slave cargo, he was acting quite properly, according to Cuban law.

Well, almost properly. If the slaves had been what the bill of lading said they were, it would have been a legal transaction. Under the laws of Cuba it was perfectly proper for any slaveowner to move his slaves as he wished. But to do it, he must have a clearance from the office of the governor general. The clearance stipulated that these slaves were *ladinos,* which meant they were slaves who had been brought into Cuba before 1820 (when the importation ceased) or were slaves actually born in Cuba. There was no particular difficulty in getting the certificate showing that the slaves were *ladinos.* The governor general's men simply collected their fees and did not bother to look at the slaves. Then the slaveowners were free to transfer them as they wished around the island.

Had anyone wished to check on the matter, it would have been simple enough to discover that the slaves were not *ladinos.* How could a slave live for nineteen years in Cuba without learning a word of Spanish? These slaves spoke the language of West Central Africa,

Many of the slaves on the *Amistad* were branded like this

not just one language, but several of them, and an observer would have discovered that many of them could not understand each other, let alone their white masters. The three little girls bought by Montez understood only the Spanish they had learned in the few days they had been in Cuba.

Toward the end of June, the *L'Amistad* was loaded with her general cargo, including spices, raisins, extracts, beans, meat, liquors, buttons, fabrics, and a shipment of long flat knives for use in the fields of sugarcane. Captain Ferrar did not want his schooner soiled by the human cargo more than necessary, so the slaves were the last items to be loaded. The ship had no accommodations for them, so that they were to be kept on deck, except at night, when they would be locked in the cargo hold. The little girls were given the run of the cabins.

On June 27 the ship moved out of Havana harbor, bound around the island for the port of Guanaja. The crew consisted of the captain, his cabin boy, Antonio, a mulatto who spoke Spanish and a mixture of the West African dialects used by the slaves, and three sailors.

The voyage began routinely, with the slaves stowed in the hold until the ship sailed, then brought on deck for air, and given food and water. The cabin boy began talking to them in a mixture of African languages, and one of the slaves spoke to him more than the others. This slave was a stocky, powerful young man from the interior named Tsingbe, who was the son of a chief in his own country beyond the Mandingo land.

Where were they going? asked Tsingbe.

To the other end of the island, said the mulatto.

What was going to happen to them? asked Tsingbe.

Oh, said the cabin boy airily, they would probably be eaten. He laughed uproariously at his own joke.

The Africans did not take the boy's words as a joke. At least one of them, a middle-aged man from deep in the interior of Africa, had the filed teeth that often denoted the cannibal tribes. And all the Africans knew something of cannibalism. Many accepted the mulatto's statement at face value.

When the slaves were put below deck that night, Tsingbe began to discuss their problem with several of the others, and they agreed that their plight could not be more desperate.

Then they ought to do something about it, said Tsingbe with an air of authority.

What could they do to save themselves?

Searching the hold for weapons, the slaves came upon cane knives—long and sharp on the edges, with straight ends. That night, as the little ship sailed around the corner of Cuba, the blacks armed themselves, and Tsingbe led the others in a stealthy move up the ladder to the hatch. They opened the hatch, stepped on deck, and made their way to the cabins.

On deck, the first man they encountered was the ship's cook, and Tsingbe swung his cane knife as the man screamed out that the slaves were loose. The cook did not scream again; his lifeless body fell to the deck.

Swiftly, Tsingbe and the others moved toward the captain's cabin. Captain Ferrar came out, eyes heavy with sleep just in time to catch a blow across his head that nearly severed it from his body. He slumped, bleeding.

Terrified, the other two crewman took the single ship's boat and began rowing silently, swiftly for the shore. The cabin boy, babbling, pleaded for his life, and he was spared because he was the link between the slaves and Ruiz and Montez, who must be saved, since some white men had to be kept alive to help the slaves find their way home.

The slaves threatened Ruiz and locked him in his cabin. They threatened Montez, until he admitted that he could sail a ship, and then they put him at the wheel and told him to sail them toward Africa, using the cabin boy as an interpreter.

The blacks then went down and freed the others. The slaves then began dressing themselves from the bolts of cloth. They broke open the raisins the ship was carrying and the spices and the extracts. Some drank so much of the alcoholic extracts that they became stupid and delirious. Not Tsingbe. He stood over Captain Montez, threatening the Spaniard with death if he made a false move.

Thereafter, for many, many days, Captain Montez steered the ship east into the rising sun by day, and then, guided by the stars, back west toward the Americas at night, when the blacks could not tell where he was going.

As the days passed, the ship became short of water, and what food they had soon gave out, so the blacks were reduced to a diet of beans and spices. They could not manage the sails properly, so the new canvas became dirty and torn, and after several weeks all that was left was the jib forestay.

So the *L'Amistad* drifted and sailed and drifted, the situation growing desperate, until finally in August she came in on the far eastern end of Long Island, New York, between Montauk Point and Gardiner's Island. There the blacks anchored the ship, and Tsingbe and several of the others took gold pieces from the captain's trunk and went ashore with casks, to gather water and to trade for food. The people were afraid of these blacks, and most of them shut their houses and would not open their doors. The blacks collected a few chickens, some eggs, and some bread, but little else.

Then, on August 28, 1839, Lieutenant Thomas R. Gedney, sailing in these waters, in command of the U.S. Navy brig *Washington,* charting the area between the island and the point came upon the long, black schooner, so ragged and so strange that she aroused his suspicions. He thought she might be a smuggling ship, plying her trade openly in these usually deserted waters. Gedney sent a boat with six men to the ship, under Lieutenant Richard W. Meade, and Passed Midshipman David D. Porter. They boarded the vessel and found the blacks, many of them sick and weak. Ruiz and Montez came to them immediately, and Montez embraced the lieutenant so fervently that Meade drew his pistol, thinking the older man meant him harm. But Ruiz explained in English that they were captives of the blacks, who had killed the captain and the cook.

As they were gaining this information, they saw the blacks of the landing party on the beach. Midshipman Porter was sent ashore with four men to arrest these blacks. He caught them as they were rowing for the ship and, drawing his pistol, brought them aboard the schooner under guard. Tsingbe, who was one of them, leaped overboard. He was wearing a belt that contained 300 gold doubloons, it was said. He swam, but was captured and brought back to the ship. (Whatever happened to the doubloons was never discovered by the authorities.)

Lieutenant Gedney heard the stories of his officers and decided that he would take the ship into port and claim salvage rights against her and the cargo. He went to New London where state authorities in Connecticut might be expected to take a lenient view.

In New London a federal district judge held an inquiry and puzzled over what was to be done. The Spaniards were quickly in touch with their minister, and he demanded the return of the ship and its cargo to Havana. The implication was that Tsingbe and the other slaves would there be tried for mutiny and murder, and would be summarily executed.

The United States had a treaty with Spain covering maritime affairs. And the Spanish claimed that this was nothing more than a matter of property—the slaves were property, too, they said. But the Anti-Slavery Society and other Abolitionist groups took an immediate interest in this case. They held that the American government could not treat these human beings as property—that they were not *ladinos* or old-time slaves, but Africans who had been kidnapped and who had a perfect right to fight for their liberty.

The blacks were taken to New Haven and lodged in the jail there, where they became curiosities for all New England to come and see. They were taken out for exercise on the town green across from the jailhouse, and hundreds of people came to watch.

President Van Buren was inclined to yield to the Spanish claims, but the uproar became so furious that the case had to go to trial, and after many delays it was tried in the federal courts in Hartford. (The blacks were taken to Hartford, some by boat and some by coach, and they were lodged in that area.)

The case went on for two years, but still it was not settled. It finally went to the United States Supreme Court. There the arguments were long and filled with technicalities—except for one argument. That was the plea made by John Quincy Adams, United States representative from Massachusetts, and former president of the United States (1825–29). Adams was asked by the Abolitionists to take the case, and he did so. He appealed to the court on the grounds of humanity, in behalf of the slaves, and his appeal was widely publicized.

In the end, the United States Supreme Court determined that the blacks were not *ladinos* as claimed, but had been illegally kidnapped Africans and ordered them sent back to Africa.

The *Amisted* Affair engendered much controversy. At one time, the federal authorities were hoping to send the blacks back to Havana before an appeal could be filed. They did not know that the Abolitionists were planning to seize the ship and save the Africans if they did so. But finally the Africans were sent back to Africa in a ship chartered for that purpose by the Abolitionists. The Spaniards continued to make claims against the American government for taking away their slaves, but these claims were never paid. The Africans simply melted back into the green jungles of equatorial Africa, except for Tsingbe, who went home and became an important man, engaging in slavery himself.

15

Attempts to Free the Slaves

In the summer of 1834 slavery was outlawed throughout the British Empire, and thereafter several incidents arose between American slaveowners and the British government of the West Indian Islands over the treatment of the black people.

One case was that of the *Enterprise* which, early in 1834, was carrying a cargo of slaves from the District of Columbia to New Orleans, when bad weather forced her into Bermuda. There the blacks of Bermuda brought legal action to free the slaves aboard the *Enterprise,* and the courts held in their favor.

In October, 1841, the ship *Creole* sailed from Richmond for New Orleans carrying a cargo of 135 slaves. Off Nassau the blacks rebelled, led by a slave known as Madison Washington, who had once escaped but had been returned to captivity, and was now being sold. In the uprising one white seaman was killed. The ship was captured by a British man-of-war and taken into Nassau, where the slaves were declared to be free.

But these were not the only efforts to free the slaves. Some had begun much, much earlier. At the end of the American Revolution Britain found herself with an increasing number of blacks in English and Canadian colonies. Nearly all these men had been freed in one way or another. Some were escaped slaves. Some were freedmen who had served in the British Navy. Some were freedmen who lived in the West Indies where they were causing considerable trouble on the plantations, even banding together as gangs of robbers, particularly in Jamaica.

Several Englishmen suggested the formation of a new British colony in Africa, using these blacks as a nucleus. This, they felt, might solve the problem. And it was done. In 1787 the ship *Nautilus* was purchased by a group of philanthropists and sailed for Africa bearing a cargo of 400 blacks who were going to start a new colony. They bought the Sierra Leone colony site and set up their new home. Soon other blacks came from Canada and the West Indies, and so the idea of a free black state took root.

Americans saw what was happening in Sierra Leone, and to some this seemed the answer to the problem of slavery in the United States. Actually, in America, it was more the problem of the blacks, and the freed blacks in particular, than the problem of slavery.

In 1800 the Virginia legislature suggested the purchase of foreign lands where "obnoxious" and "dangerous" persons might be sent. The legislators were referring to black persons. Some other state legislatures talked of sending blacks to Haiti; some, of carving a part out of the new Louisiana Territory to give to the blacks. In 1816 Henry Clay led in the formation of the American Colonization Society, whose purpose was to send the freed blacks to Africa. He became a vice-president of the society and so did Andrew Jackson.

In 1819, when the president and Congress were preparing to give at least token support to the British effort to suppress the slave trade, the Colonization Society cooperated and helped establish a place in Africa where slaves freed by the American Africa Squadron might be delivered. The ship *Elizabeth* was chartered by the government, in cooperation with the society. Eighty-six freed slaves were persuaded to go to Africa, and a black minister, the Reverend Samuel Bacon, was appointed by the government to go with them. They sailed from Boston on February 6, 1820, and landed on the African coast at Sherboro, where a black named Kizel had come earlier from New Bedford and established a small colony.

The Sherboro colony did not prosper. The American blacks quickly contracted fever, and many succumbed to it, Bacon among them. The remaining blacks left and went to Sierra Leone, which was already an established community.

But a colony had to be established, for the Americans were beginning to capture slave ships and cargoes of Africans and had to have some place to send them.

Captain R. F. Stockton was sent out in the schooner *Alligator* to explore the African coast and find a place for a colony. He selected Cape Mesurado, and soon a piece of land between the Mesurado and Junk rivers was bought from the African rulers of the area.

The colony struggled. For several years it lay between the devil and the sea—the devil represented by the black African chiefs who dealt in slaves, and the sea by the slavers who came to buy. There were slave stations and slave colonies on both sides of the free colony. The free colonists were forced to fight for survival, and they did, attacking the chiefs, and winning, and then attacking the slave settlement called Tradetown. They destroyed the slave factories there and blew up the barracoons with gunpowder. Thus, Liberia came into being, and it survived.

In 1834 Maryland citizens formed another colonization society and sent out a force in the brig *Ann.* They established a settlement at Cape Palmas. The Pennsylvania Colonization Society sent 126 emigrants, most of them freed slaves, to Bassa Cova to set up a new colony. There were many colonists now and much rivalry among them. In 1836 a black man named Thomas Buchanan united the colonies under a government at Monrovia. Liberia asked for American protection—to become an American colony—but the United States government wanted no colonies and refused the offer. Buchanan died and was succeeded by a black named Joseph J. Roberts, a very statesmanlike figure, who completed the establishment of the nation and made Lib-

A slave is examined before purchase

eria an independent state on August 24, 1847. At this time the emigrant population, mostly from the United States, came to about 5,000 people, while there were some 10,000 native Africans in the country. (By the 1970s the population of independent Liberia had risen to 1,200,000.) All things considered, the Liberian experiment could not be considered a very great success. The liberated slaves and freemen who went back had an unfortunate tendency to take advantage of their neighbors, and there were reports of slaving and slave-trading in Liberia as late as the 1920s. Monrovia was settled, and the rest of the country was controlled by an American elite that did not respond very well to the needs of Africa or Africans. The proof of it is in the position of Liberia today. By all counts, given the supposed head start of American freedom and American capital, Liberia should be far ahead of its black neighbor states, at least economically. It is not ahead either economically or politically, but rather lags behind most of its neighbors.

16

The Arrogant Americans

In the eighteenth century the slave trade was a very important part of New England commerce. The prohibition of the trade in 1807 made it more difficult and dangerous, except that the coastwise trade made an exception. Anyone with a ship of forty tons or more could transport slaves for sale from one American port to another by delivering manifests to the collectors of the ports on sailing and arriving. And so a strange American slave trade grew up between the breeding stations in Virginia, which specialized in raising slaves, and the big marketplace in New Orleans.

The slave trade in the last years before the Civil War became a truly big business, as is indicated by the story of a slave-trader named Charles Lamar, of Savannah. Lamar proposed to raise $300,000. Of this he would use $150,000 to buy the *Vigo*, a 1,750-ton steamer with an iron screw. He would stock her with small arms and put six fixed guns on deck, so she could fight off all comers

—British or American Africa Squadron ships, or piratical raiders. The cost of the arms would be $50,000; supplies and food for crew and slaves would cost $25,-000; and $75,000 cash would be needed for the purchase of the slave cargo.

The *Vigo* would steam to Africa at eleven knots, under command of one of the finest American naval officers, Lamar said. She would pick up 1,200 slaves. These would be sold in the market for $650 each, bringing in $780,000 or a profit of $480,000 which would be divided among the crew and owners. And that did not include the ship. They would still have her completely paid off for another voyage.

The *Vigo* arrangement did not work out, but it was most certainly not the only ship considered, or purchased, for the slave trade.

Among the latter-day slavers of America, perhaps the most infamous was the *Wanderer*, a handsome yacht. She was built in 1857 for J. D. Johnson, a member of the New York Yacht Club. She was 104 feet overall, 26.5 feet in the beam, and she drew 10.5 feet of water. Her mainmast reached 84 feet above deck, and above that was her topmast, another 35 feet. She was slender and fast, the pride of her owner. Nevertheless, he sold her to Captain W. C. Corrie, and Captain Corrie was duly elected to the Yacht Club. Soon Captain Corrie went sailing off to the south in his new yacht, flying the burgee of the New York Yacht Club, one of the most respected in the world.

Captain Corrie did not tell his friends at the Yacht Club, but he had a definite idea in mind when he

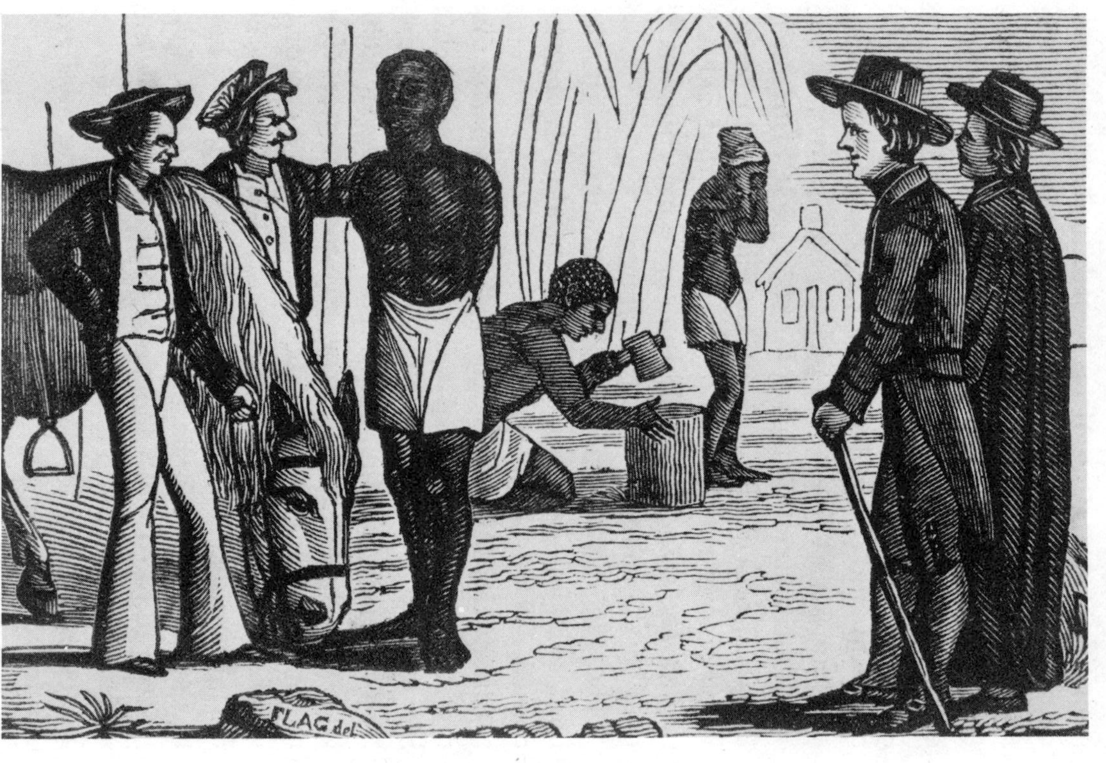

Slave being traded for horses

bought the *Wanderer.* Soon he was in Charleston, and soon after that he had a slaver outfit in the hold of the *Wanderer.* Accompanied by Captain Egbert Farnham, an adventurer of some renown, Captain Corrie cleared Charleston harbor bound for Trinidad, he said. But he did not add that Trinidad was not his ultimate destination. The ship left Trinidad and appeared at St. Helena, still flying the New York Yacht Club burgee. Next, she was seen on the Congo River—a strange place for an American yacht!

On the Congo the *Wanderer* encountered the British warship *Medusa.* Captain Corrie ran alongside and hailed. The British saw the yacht club flag and were impressed. Corrie entertained them and invited them to inspect the *Wanderer* to see if she was a slaver. The British officers declined the invitation, laughing uproariously at the idea that his luxury yacht might be a slave ship. And with the New York Yacht Club flag aloft, at that!

The *Medusa* had business along the coast, and she had to sail away. Then the *Wanderer* moved upriver, hunting the barracoons where she could load the slave cargo. The captain was working for a syndicate, which included among its members Charles Lamar of Savannah.

The *Wanderer* took on 750 slaves, most of them young people between thirteen and eighteen years of age. She sailed for the American coast, arriving about December 1, 1858.

She had to get up the Savannah River in view of the

authorities. Obviously this could not be done in daytime, so the ship crept in at night and went up the river to the big swamp where she was concealed. The crew then got in touch with Lamar in Savannah.

Lamar was equal to the problem. He announced that he was giving an entertainment for all the officers and men of the fort, and he did so, making as sure as he could that every man drank more than he should. While the party was at its height, the *Wanderer* stole up the river, past the fort, to Lamar's plantation, where the slaves were finally unloaded.

But the federal district attorney had heard of the coming of the slave ship, and he began to move. The *Wanderer* was seized. Lamar tried to bribe all those concerned, but it was not easy, because the publicity was too great. Soon other officials were involved. Doctors came to examine the blacks and announced that they were Africans and not native American blacks. Lamar had shipped some to other planters, who took them and then refused to give them up.

But soon Captain Corrie was arrested, and so was Lamar. The latter kept trying to bribe all the officials, offering a witness as much as $5,000 if he would not testify. But the case moved on, and Lamar decided that if he was convicted he would go to Cuba.

Eventually, Lamar apparently did bribe enough people, for the slavers escaped, although the *Wanderer* was sold at auction by the government. She brought about a quarter of her value and then was put in service as a merchant schooner.

Slaves in South Carolina

Lamar profited nicely, despite all his troubles. The slaves were sold for $600 to $700 each, the captain and crew were paid off and the syndicate shared the profits. Lamar was already thinking about a new venture. This time he planned to send a ship to China to buy coolies who would cost $12 each and could be sold for $350 apiece in Cuba. The plan was later abandoned as too dangerous.

The *Wanderer* did not remain honest for long. In 1859 she was again in the hands of slavers and made another voyage to Africa, back up the Congo, and picked up 600 blacks, whom she brought to the Georgia coast. Trying to enter the Jekyll Creek between Jekyll and Cumberland Islands, she was struck by a squall and ran aground. Some of the blacks panicked and threw themselves overboard, to be drowned. Later, she was freed, and the remainder of the slaves were landed safely and sold again at a high profit.

When the New York Yacht Club learned of the Lamar affair, the name of the *Wanderer* was stricken from the list of ships of the squadron, and Captain Corrie was expelled from the club forever. The *Wanderer* was making ready for another slave voyage when the Civil War began, and she was sold to the Confederate government, to become a pilot and scouting boat. She was eventually captured by the Union forces and used as a revenue cutter at Pensacola. After the war she was sold into the coconut trade of Honduras, where she remained until driven ashore on Cape Henry.

In the last few months of the slave trade in America,

it was estimated that 15,000 slaves were brought in to the southern states. Some slavers prospered, but some, like Captain Timothy Meagher, did not. Captain Meagher brought 175 slaves from Africa to the Mobile River in the fall of 1858. But the news of his landing got out, and various officials rushed to claim the slaves and the prize money for capturing them. Captain Meagher had laid out $100,000 on his voyage, but he was able to sell only twenty-five of the slaves before the rest were taken. If he broke even on the voyage he was lucky.

As the slavery issue became more and more of a divisive force between North and South, the southerners seemed to lose concern for cost entirely. Slaves *were* expensive, no doubt about it. Some of them sold for as much as $1,800 just before the war. So the southerners appealed for the reopening of the slave trade with Africa. Such resolutions were passed in many southern legislatures and even reached the floor of Congress before the abhorrent idea was rejected.

17

The End of the Western Slave Trade

On the eve of the Civil War Britain was so annoyed by America's thwarting of the agreements to end the trade that it was suggested in the House of Commons that a Cuban Squadron be sent out. Another suggestion was that the Congo area be sealed off and that Britain annex some of the territories along the Slave Coast. The British grew more annoyed as they learned in 1860 that some eighty-five slave ships were fitted out in a year in New York harbor alone.

In February, 1861, Lord Palmerston arose in Parliament and spoke against the Cuban trade, making no bones about the fact that this was an American abomination. And, the British claimed, it was not the southerners, by and large, who were involved in this traffic in human flesh, but the northerners. Actually, it was both.

But a month later, Abraham Lincoln was inaugurated

as president of the United States. A few weeks later the Civil War began. In October, 1861, the British Admiralty received a remarkable communication from the United States, by way of the Foreign Office. United States Secretary of State Seward announced that in the future the British should search any American vessel that they suspected to be engaged in the slave trade. Further, the United States government announced that New York would no longer be a major port for slavers. All slave ships would be stopped and confiscated.

Events were moving very rapidly. One victim of the times—in a way an unfortunate victim—was an American captain, Nathaniel Gordon. Captain Gordon was an old-time slave-trader from Portland, Maine, who had been sailing in recent years out of New York harbor on his successful and profitable voyages.

In the summer of 1860 Captain Gordon had taken the ship *Erie* to Havana and fitted her out as a slaver. He went to the mouth of the Congo River and then sailed forty-five miles upstream, where he traded a cargo of West Indian rum for 890 slaves, most of them boys and girls. On August 7, 1860, he sailed for Cuba. Unfortunately for him, fifty miles offshore he encountered the U.S.S. *Mohican,* of the American Africa Squadron, and soon the *Erie* was run down and captured.

The ship was first taken to Liberia, where the slaves were freed. Captain Gordon and the *Erie* were then taken under guard to New York for trial. In the fall of

1860, just before the presidential election, the ship was condemned and sold for $7,800, a very good price for a 500-ton vessel in that time.

Now, for the first time in American history, there was a real clamor for a trial under the law of 1820, which declared slave-trading to be the equivalent of piracy, punishable by death. On November 6, 1861, Captain Gordon was brought to trial. Two days later the jury returned with a verdict: guilty.

On November 30, a motion was made for a new trial. The retrial was denied, and Gordon was sentenced to be hanged by the neck until he was dead.

Some friends and advocates of slavery tried to save Gordon. After all, scores of captains had been caught earlier, and nobody had ever been hanged under the law of 1820. But the times had changed. The Civil War had brought an end to open sympathy with slavery in the North. There was no one, really, to defend the captain; he was a victim of the times.

President Lincoln was asked for clemency. He held up the execution for two weeks, then decided that the case was simple and clear and that Gordon must die for his crimes.

There was action. Governors and friends appealed in Gordon's behalf. It was rumored that he would be rescued by a mob. But Lincoln refused to listen to appeals and would not accept telegrams containing appeals. A guard of eighty Marines from the Navy Yard came to New York City Prison.

On the evening of February 20, 1862, Captain Gordon wrote a few letters and went to sleep about one o'clock in the morning. He awakened two hours later, and from some secret hiding place brought forth a fatal dose of strychnine and swallowed it. As he began to feel the effects, he shouted at his guards: "I've cheated you!"

The guards were swift, and doctors came immediately. They pumped out Captain Gordon's stomach and saved him. Just before noon the federal marshal came to the cell and read the death sentence. Captain Gordon was now composed, although bitter against his sentence for a crime so many others had committed in the past, without being punished. At noon he went to the gallows, and in a few moments he was dead.

So, by this time slavery and the slave trade was very nearly dead in the western world. The town of Lagos fell before the British might, and in 1861 the Lagos territory was annexed by Britain, ostensibly to put an end to the slave trade in the Bight of Africa. At the same time a British force went inland to punish the king of Porto Novo, west of Lagos, because that ruler had broken his promise and was engaging in the slave trade once again.

In 1862 there were still slaves traded, between Africa, Cuba, and South America. The trade was much curtailed, to be sure, by the American Civil War, but it continued to exist. Britain decided to act. Now the one big problem was the Kingdom of Dahomey, whose warlike ruler would brook no interference with his right to deal in slaves. Britain sent naval officers to negotiate with him, but old King Gelele refused to discuss the matter. If he could not sell his captives as slaves, he said, he would simply cut off their heads.

He was adamant, this old African king, but it did him little good. By 1863 the Confederates were feeling the pinch of war, and there simply was no more slave trade with America. The Emancipation Proclamation made it quite clear that there would never be again. In 1864 the British blockaded the African coast with a number of cruisers, the kingdom of Dahomey was sealed off from the sea, and the Atlantic slave trade was coming to an end. In 1865 the first Spanish slaver was executed under the laws of his own government: Two years later the Africa Squadron of the Royal Navy was in the process of dissolution, and in 1868 the Mixed Commission was dissolved because there were no more cases involving slaves and slavers.

Slavery still existed, however. Cuban slavery was alleviated in 1870 when the Spanish parliament passed a law that every slave who reached the age of sixty should be free and that all unborn children should be free. That was a gradual way of emancipating the slaves. There were half a million slaves in Cuba; ten years later the institution was practically extinct.

In Brazil, slavery was finally abolished by the parliament in 1871 on a gradual basis, and then absolutely in 1888 when an estimated 700,000 people were freed.

The trade in East Africa centered around Zanzibar for a long time. In 1872 Britain sent a powerful mission there to close down the slave trade, and officially this was accomplished, as far as Zanzibar was concerned, in

1876. But the trading in human flesh continued—the African coast is long and filled with little bays, and the Arab dhows could come in quietly and slip away by night.

The big difference came in 1885 when thirteen nations of Europe and the United States pledged themselves to stamp out the slave trade, partially by policing, and partially by prohibiting trade in guns and ammunition other than flintlocks and black powder. Still the trade continued in Egypt until 1898 when it was suppressed by Lord Kitchener. Five years later, or so, slave-trading was stopped in Nigeria, the Congo, and Nyasaland. However, the excuse of suppression of the slave trade in the last years of the nineteenth century brought into play another force nearly as destructive: colonialism. Britain, France, and Belgium in particular used the existence of the slave trade as an excuse to take control of new areas of territory and to put down Muslim leaders who engaged freely in the trade.

By 1910 the more or less thorough control of Africa by Europeans, and the more or less equally thorough control of slavery had been achieved. But actually, one of the reasons the nations of the world looked upon Ethiopia askance and set the stage for Italian conquest in that country was the existence of slavery in Ethiopia up to the 1930s.

Nor was slavery so easy to stamp out in the Muslim world, where it was a very definite part of the social system. The continued independence of Muslim leaders in the deserts meant the continuation of slavery, and there was a lively traffic in slaves along the ports of the Red Sea where few European cruisers called. The League of Nations established several standing and special committees to deal with slavery in the 1920s and 1930s. In 1936 Ibn Saud of Saudi Arabia, whose kingdom was one of the most flagrant offenders against the slavery laws, decreed that no more slaves should be imported into his territory by sea and that by land only duly certified slaves could be imported. This act was an attempt to stop the illegal slave trade. It did a great deal to put an end to the trade in Saudi Arabia, but Ibn Saud and his successors did not and do not control all the Arabian peninsula or Arab lands, where slavery is still a part of the structure. Slavery still existed in the world in the 1970s in sufficient degree to be a concern of the United Nations Commission on Human Rights, although as world problems go it is a very minor one. But not until the little kingdoms of the world can be brought to accept international law and mores will slavery be stamped out completely in the world.

Suggested Reading

Adventures of an African Slaver, being a true account of the life of Captain Theodore Canot, trader in gold, ivory, slaves, on the coast of Guinea: His own story as told in the year 1854 to Brantz Mayer. Edited and with an introduction by Malcolm Cowley, Albert and Charles Boni, New York, 1928

The American Slave Trade, an account of its origin, growth and suppression, by John R. Spears, Charles Scribner's Sons, New York, 1900

Black Cargoes, a History of the Atlantic Slave Trade, 1518–1865, by Daniel P. Mannix in collaboration with Malcolm Cowley, Viking Press, New York, 1962

Black Mother, by Basil Davidson, Atlantic–Little, Brown, Boston, 1961

The Last Years of the English Slave Trade, by Averil Mackenzie-Grieve, Augustus M. Kelley, New York, 1968

The Navy and the Slave Trade, the suppression of the African Slave Trade in the nineteenth century, by Christopher Lloyd, Longmans Green and Co., New York, 1949

Slave Ships and Slaving, by George Francis Dow, Marine Research Society, Salem, Mass., 1927

Index